T0271238

# MANAGING ACADEMIC LIBRARIES

# CHANDOS

## INFORMATION PROFESSIONAL SERIES

Series Editor: Ruth Rikowski
(email: Rikowskigr@aol.com)

Chandos' new series of books is aimed at the busy information professional. They have been specially commissioned to provide the reader with an authoritative view of current thinking. They are designed to provide easy-to-read and (most importantly) practical coverage of topics that are of interest to librarians and other information professionals. If you would like a full listing of current and forthcoming titles, please visit www.chandospublishing.com.

New authors: We are always pleased to receive ideas for new titles; if you would like to write a book for Chandos, please contact Dr Glyn Jones on g.jones.2@elsevier.com or telephone +44 (0) 1865 843000.

# MANAGING ACADEMIC LIBRARIES
## Principles and Practice

**SUSAN HIGGINS**

With a contribution by Maryam Derakhshan

ELSEVIER

Amsterdam • Boston • Cambridge • Heidelberg
London • New York • Oxford • Paris • San Diego
San Francisco • Singapore • Sydney • Tokyo
Chandos Publishing is an imprint of Elsevier

CHANDOS
PUBLISHING

Chandos Publishing is an imprint of Elsevier
50 Hampshire Street, 5th Floor, Cambridge, MA 02139, United States
The Boulevard, Langford Lane, Kidlington, OX5 1GB, United Kingdom

**Notices**
Knowledge and best practice in this field are constantly changing. As new research and experience broaden our understanding, changes in research methods, professional practices, or medical treatment may become necessary.

Practitioners and researchers must always rely on their own experience and knowledge in evaluating and using any information, methods, compounds, or experiments described herein. In using such information or methods they should be mindful of their own safety and the safety of others, including parties for whom they have a professional responsibility.

To the fullest extent of the law, neither the Publisher nor the authors, contributors, or editors, assume any liability for any injury and/or damage to persons or property as a matter of products liability, negligence or otherwise, or from any use or operation of any methods, products, instructions, or ideas contained in the material herein.

**Library of Congress Cataloging-in-Publication Data**
A catalog record for this book is available from the Library of Congress

**British Library Cataloguing-in-Publication Data**
A catalogue record for this book is available from the British Library

ISBN: 978-1-84334-621-0 (print)
ISBN: 978-1-78063-311-4 (online)

For information on all Chandos Publishing publications
visit our website at https://www.elsevier.com/

Working together
to grow libraries in
developing countries

www.elsevier.com • www.bookaid.org

*Publisher:* Glyn Jones
*Acquisition Editor:* Glyn Jones
*Senior Editorial Project Manager:* Kattie Washington
*Production Project Manager:* Debasish Ghosh
*Designer:* Vicky Pearson Esser

Typeset by TNQ Books and Journals

*This book is dedicated to my parents, Thomas E. Higgins Sr.
and Luthenea Waddell.*

*A special thank you is extended to Maryam Derakhshan, Department of Library
and Information Science, University of Tarbiat Modares, Iran.
Professor Derakhshan wrote Chapter 3 entitled "*Library and Information
Science as a Discipline.*"*

# CONTENTS

# ABOUT THE AUTHOR

Susan E. Higgins is currently an Adjunct Instructor for San Jose State University School of Information as well as the University of Arizona School of Information. She taught at the University of Southern Mississippi School of Library and Information Science, Charles Sturt University in Wagga Wagga, New South Wales, Australia and Nanyang Technological University's Wee Kim Wee School of Communication and Information in Singapore.

She has previously published a book with Chandos entitled *Youth Services and Public Libraries,* which has been translated into Serbian. Her research interests include collection management, academic librarianship, and youth services and resources in libraries.

# INTRODUCTION

Because academic libraries are at the heart of the college or university they serve, managing them is inexplicably intertwined with management of the institution itself. The concept of sustainability in academic libraries is today's focus, an international focus, and a return to the foundations of managing academic libraries well is essential to understanding this concept. Anne Sibbel (2009) wrote, "higher education curricula need offer experiences which develop graduate attributes of self-efficacy, the capacity for effective advocacy and interdisciplinary collaboration, as well as raise awareness of social and moral responsibilities associated with professional practice." Such learning for professional dispositions is essential for the academic librarian of today. Knowledge of the institution's curriculum is, as always, essential. Collaboration with faculty provides enriched learning experiences for students. The academic librarian is grounded in the culture of the institution that employs them, and with this knowledge, can open doors and minds. The management of academic libraries must also be deliberate and sustained, and intended to develop support for the library and staff over time. In order to serve their users, academic librarians need to possess background knowledge of the history of higher education as well as how academic cultures within their own institutions have evolved. Sustainability in management is a holistic idea addressing the environment, the culture, and the economic issues of universities. It is at odds with the theory of managerialism. Managerialism "glorifies hierarchy, technology, and the role of the manager in modern society" (Edwards, 1998). Edwards (1998) also wrote, "Put simply, the values and assumptions associated with managerialism provide broad targets for those who believe that public administrators should be more active in defining political goals and redressing social injustice." A return to the centrality of learning and reading will counteract managerialism and social injustice. It makes sense to judge universities on how well students are learning and reading and how well administrators, whether in the United States, Australia, the United Kingdom, or China, are responding to such a culture. Maurice Line, the British former university librarian and Director-General of the British Library wrote that the division in universities between teaching, the library, Information and Communications Technology, and educational technology is increasingly meaningless, and the importance of learning how to learn should lead the partnership between teachers and librarians. Line believed that the entire university should be restructured to meet societal and individual needs. Bill Crowley also linked learning and reading to the definition of value understood by public and government leaders. Educated people will help solve societal problems. David Boud (2000) wrote, "Lifelong assessment is a necessary feature of lifelong learning for a learning society. It is only when we can view it in formative terms that we can avoid assessment becoming a form of incarceration" (Boud, p. 2). Too often assessment is a form of incarceration because poor management and supervision makes it so. Ultimately, the social injustice of isolation from the real goals of higher education, facilitating thinking, responsible, and collaborative human beings is lost. As James Dewey wrote, "Education is not preparation for life; education is life itself" http://www.brainyquote.com/quotes/quotes/j/johndewey154060.html.

This book is organized in chapters to emphasize the importance of managing academic libraries with the appropriate demeanor and with rich resources. It explores the universals of the management of academic libraries because it is intended for an international audience. The premise is that an understanding of what is to be managed will focus on individual and ultimately societal needs. For example, in a university library, collaboration between the library's collection development officers and the faculty who set collection parameters through their respective subjects, research, and interests is critical in building a collection that supports the curriculum and serves the students and faculty. The use of technology in academic libraries supports the superordinate goals of university education itself.

# CHAPTER 1

# Managing the Centrality of Learning, Reading, Individual Inquiry, and Public Service

## 1.1 INFORMATION VERSUS READING

T. S. Eliot famously asked, "Where is the wisdom we have lost in knowledge? Where is the knowledge we have lost in information?" Librarians rightly embrace the concept of information, but the scholarly character of our profession makes us care about leading library users to knowledge and wisdom. This chapter explores the centrality of reading and learning, of individual inquiry and the obligation of public service, all intangibles of the caring profession. Public service remains the essential goal of academic librarians and is part of the current discussion of "student success," the raison d'être of academic librarians everywhere.

The study of public, school, and academic libraries has generally declined in schools of library science, whereas the emphasis on information science has increased (Higgins, 2003). The decline in library science professions has continued for a decade due to a weak library job market and hiring freezes. Although the impact of information technology in academic libraries has been profound, the interaction between a reader and a text is not the same as the human–computer interaction. Dillon (2007) states that, "[f]or half a century, LIS has been … divided … artificially between library and information science, a division that mirrored implicit distinctions between people and technology orientations, between qualitative and quantitative methods, and between impressionist and scientific identities" (Dillon, 2007). Reading is a bridge between cultures and social groups and can be a bridge between library and information science as well.

As technology becomes more sophisticated, opportunities to support collaboration using technology have grown. Because digital

*Managing Academic Libraries*
ISBN 978-1-84334-621-0
http://dx.doi.org/10.1016/B978-1-84334-621-0.00001-7

technology continues to affect academic libraries so deeply, it has also affected the concept of reliable information and identity of the library profession. Distance education and distributed learning have changed the way people consume information, as well as their relationship with librarians. Maloney and Antelman, et al. (2010) write that academic libraries have felt threatened by "disruptive technologies," which do new things and target new users. Print material lining countless shelves is being replaced by immersive environments where students can chat in real time to learn and exchange information. They can construct 3D objects and exhibits, make presentations, and meet in virtual groups for discussion. The process of learning becomes more social. Librarians still have a role in this kind of learning, and one of them is helping people evaluate information, which is part of critical reading and thinking. The idea of purposeful reading has not changed, even as information literacy classes have become commonplace. Reading in today's academic library is socially collaborative, and the information literacy skill set continues to evolve.

Campbell (2006) states that,

> [a]cademic libraries are complex institutions with multiple roles and a host of related operations and services developed over the years. Yet their fundamental purpose has remained the same: to provide access to trustworthy, authoritative knowledge. Consequently, academic libraries, along with their private and governmental counterparts, have long stood unchallenged throughout the world as the primary providers of recorded knowledge and historical records. Within the context of higher education especially, when users wanted dependable information, they turned to academic libraries (p. 16).

Crowley (2008) advocates, "amending the out-of-date concept of information centrality ... to recapture—and grant equal status to— the core status of the learning and reading roles that was so well supported by library history and the original ALA accreditation efforts of the 1920s" (p. 22). Crowley recommends that "lifecycle librarianship," the "development of library services appropriate for the entire human life cycle," be practiced as a link to both the past and the future. To manage a learning organization such as an academic library, one must turn back to the power of individual inquiry and create a higher education culture that values public service. Lifecycle librarianship can help higher education adhere to its public service mission.

Reading, learning, and the creation of informed citizens are important in the history of higher education. Budd (2005) describes an important event in that history, the founding of Johns Hopkins University in Baltimore, Maryland, in 1876. Johns Hopkins was modeled on 19th century German universities, which emphasized individual inquiry (Budd, p. 27). The place of research and the model of the German university were focused on two central tenets: *Lehrfreiheit* (the freedom to teach) and *Lernfreiheit* (the freedom to learn). The freedom to teach and learn was practiced through inquiry and the personal investigation by students and professors (Budd, pp. 23–24).

Kuh and Gonyea (2003) cite three trends affecting academic libraries in the light of public accountability and financial constraints: "(1) unfettered asynchronous access to an exponentially expanding information base; (2) a shift in the focus of colleges and universities from teaching to learning; and (3) the expectation that all university functions and programs demonstrate their effectiveness" (p. 256). They found that technology has clearly made information more accessible and easier to navigate but that students still used libraries and library resources. They found that "Hispanic, Latino, and black students use library resources more frequently, whereas white students use libraries the least. Students majoring in humanities and social sciences are ... the most frequent users of the library, as are students who report two or more majors. Students with undecided majors and those majoring in business, math, and science score the lowest on the library scale. Finally, students attending baccalaureate liberal arts colleges use the library more often, whereas those attending baccalaureate general colleges and doctoral/research-extensive universities do so least often" (p. 265).

## 1.2  THE INFORMATION-LITERATE PERSON

Learning, reading, and reflection are central to the practice of academic librarianship. Learning and reading are central to the idea of an information-literate person and are rooted in individual freedom of inquiry and intellectual life. Students who use academic libraries develop the ability to think critically about the information they encounter. Their use of information to develop personal and professional competencies is fundamental to education in a global world.

Reading and learning support literacy, which in turn supports freedom of speech, expression, and the press. Intellectual freedom does not exist without literacy because intellectual freedom implies critical thinking. Molesworth, Nixon, and Scullion (2009) state that "[o]nce, under the guidance of the academic, the undergraduate had the potential to be transformed into a scholar, someone who thinks critically, but in our consumer society such 'transformation' is denied and 'confirmation' of the student as consumer is favored" (p. 277). The competitive pressures universities are now experiencing result from changes in financial support, increasing costs of education, and demand for educational services.

Dunn and Menchaca (2009) note that widespread access to information via search engines has allowed users to bypass libraries for available Web resources. Digitization initiatives have both democratized and commercialized library holdings, and academic institutions have become marginalized as primary sources of information. However, according to Milewsicz (2009), the greatest marginalization occurs because the university library is challenged to balance the life of the mind with the demands of a consumer-driven society. The digital environment is an information community, and librarians add value to the processes of information creation, dissemination, and access. The diverse material types and formats have created issues of integration, cataloguing, and navigation.

## 1.3 GLOBAL OUTLOOK

Raju and Raju (2009) write that despite the Carnegie Report (2000), which argues that, "books and their availability cannot be a priority in a continent ravaged by poverty, war, famine and HIV/AIDS," in fact, "books and information will always be a catalyst in solving a nation's problems" (p. 45). Cross (2010) proposes that librarians need to adopt the economic principle, "first do no harm." Budgets should be reviewed in terms of economic principles, student diversity, and social justice. There is a continuing tension in discussions of higher education between the goals of occupational training and of the development of the mind, of a love of ideas, and of the ability to think critically and solve problems. This tension has budgetary implications and is part of the need for universities and academic libraries to "communicate value," including the value of reading and thinking.

These issues are not just important in the United States and United Kingdom, and other industrialized areas such as Canada, Australia, and Western Europe, but also in populous countries in Asia and Africa, including India, Pakistan, Nigeria, and others. In countries like Nigeria, the idea of a "reading culture" is seen as an essential part of national development. Igwe (2011) describes the barriers to reading culture as lack of funds and information infrastructure. Aina, et al. (2011) likewise describe a situation where children may move "straight from oral to digital culture," without becoming readers. Lone (2011) explores the reading habits of college students in India. Librarians in Nigeria, India, and elsewhere are very interested in the "open access" movement and in institutional repositories, which have the potential to make more information available to more people at a lower cost, and to have a democratizing effect (Nazim and Mukherjee, 2011; Okoye and Ejikeme, 2011; and many others). These and other international authors also write of severe problems with funding and infrastructure (Ubogu and Okiy, 2011; Ayo-Sobowale and Akinyemi, 2011).

## 1.4 ACADEMIC LIBRARIES AND STUDENT SUCCESS

There can be debate on the meaning of "reading" or "literacy," but there can be no doubt that libraries are now, and have always been, institutions that enshrine reading and literacy as central aspects of their mission. Libraries were created as repositories of texts that supported learning, scholarship, and leisure. Librarianship emerged as a profession to organize and give access to information for these purposes. Librarians have acted as scholars, systematizers, teachers, helpers, and technicians.

These things are true of academic libraries in particular. Colleges and universities exist to teach critical thinking and independent inquiry, and academic libraries foster and support those goals.

Libraries are about reading, learning, and thinking. This is more the case in the present digital environment than ever.

In the past 30 years, colleges and universities have become more accountable and student centered. The focus on recruitment and retention has led to the concept of "student success." Student success includes everything that allows students to stay in school, graduate on time, enjoy their experience, and benefit from it. Elements of student success include life skills, academic skills, and emotional and financial security and support. A successful student is an educated citizen who can give back to society. Academic librarians have the opportunity to be leaders in student success, using assessment, accountability, and partnership. Academic libraries have an important role in student success and its connection to a culture of reading, thinking, and public service.

Recruitment and retention of students have been the focus of higher education for more than 20 years. Universities have focused on teaching enhancement, on educational technology, and on programs and services to support student success. Academic libraries are currently involved in conversations on campus that are focused on partnerships for student success. These partnerships include writing and tutoring centers, and many other kinds of shared spaces for collaboration, use of new media, performances, exhibits, and many other things. These "student success centers" will strengthen the role of academic libraries in reading (interacting with texts and other kinds of material) and learning, and will help create educated citizens who themselves value public service.

Libraries are also attempting to assess and document their value in student success. The Association of College and Research Libraries (American Library Association, 2012) has created a program to involve academic libraries in student success and to communicate the value of academic librarians in that success.

The traditional library services include a large print collection, which requires ordering, receiving, cataloging, processing, and database maintenance, in-person reference and instruction, multiple service points, and specialized branch libraries. The transition to the digital environment has seen the addition of extensive electronic resources, which have grown in size, stability, and interoperability. It has seen consortia collection-building, virtual reference service, and new modes of instruction. In the second decade of the 21st century, the digital environment continues to be transformative, and academic libraries are assessing trends, creating scenarios, and trying to envision and embrace radical change that will keep them relevant. The future is disintermediated and patron driven. Information is available faster, and it is portable, available from anywhere at any time.

In this transitional time and in the rapidly emerging future, how can libraries be leaders in student success and continue to support the culture of reading, individual inquiry, and the public service that is essential for an educated and literate citizenry? The answer lies in the core values and activities of libraries and librarianship. Those values include the love of scholarship and learning and the desire to foster and support those values in others. The activities that support them are the systems that provide access to information and the services that help library users find it and find their information focus.

Some may feel that libraries have abandoned the ideas of reading and individual inquiry, but these things are more central and more supported by the current digital environment. Patrons have access to a wider array of texts, but also audio and video, visual materials of all kinds, as well as archival and special collections materials, to an extent that was never possible in the past. They are immersed in the scholarly universe in a way that was unimaginable in the past. While there is still a digital divide, the current information environment has a democratizing potential that can provide access to more people and provide a richer array of resources than at any time in the past. The future of academic libraries is part of the discussion of the future of higher education and of education in general. While much of the discussion involves the exciting and rapidly changing digital environment, it is really a discussion about individual inquiry and public service, that is, the creation of educated citizens. There is a flourishing literature on the future of academic libraries, including international issues and models. How do the predictions fit in with a vision of a reading culture, a culture of inquiry? How do they contribute to student success?

The answer to this lies in the programs and services libraries provide as well as in the organizational characteristics of libraries. Academic libraries cannot provide services that support teaching and research unless they embrace the idea of continuous learning as a part of their own organization. That may mean the implementation of models of organizational development such as the learning organization.

The Association for College and Research Libraries (ACRL; 2012) urges libraries to prove and communicate their value. This means being willing and able to assess programs and use the results of assessment to make the case for support from administrators and governing bodies. One impact that academic libraries are attempting to demonstrate is their beneficial effect on student success. Libraries are trying to demonstrate that the funds they receive are worth it, to provide valuable scholarly information resources, and to teach students, faculty, and administrators that all information is not "free on the Internet."

At the same time, the Internet does provide a great deal of freely available material for learning, including texts to read, as well as video, audio, and many different kinds of interactive learning experiences such as courses, tutorials, etc. The open access material on the Web causes us to question the nature of authority, ways of validating knowledge, and the idea of reliable information. It also allows us to embrace a democratic and participative vision of society. To some extent, the creation and development of the Web parallels the creation of public libraries, where learning is open to all. Nevertheless, libraries also provide access to costly licensed material whose contents have been validated by scholars or publishers.

## 1.5 THEORIES OF READING, LEARNING, AND LITERACY

Libraries provide extensive collections for reading. Reading is implicitly associated with learning. There are a number of different models of learning, and, individuals have preferred learning styles. The ideas of reading culture and individual inquiry are ones that embrace and use technology. The digital realm is a place where those things can flourish. The present environment is one that supports and encourages multiple literacies and multiple learning styles. "Reading" does not refer only to text, and there are theories of reading and literacy as well. One of the ways that the role of libraries in student success can be demonstrated is by looking at the correlation of factors like retention, time to graduation, grade point average, and so on, with use of library resources.

There are a number of theories of learning, of which the cognitive and constructivist are most relevant to the role of libraries. Cognitive theories view learning as a mental process. Constructivist models do not deny that there is cognitive activity by learners but view learning as a more complex and varied process, in which learners do various things to take knowledge that is imparted to them (by a lecture, a book, a video, etc.) to construct meaning for themselves.

There are various inventories of learning styles. Commonly accepted styles include verbal, aural, visual, social, physical, solitary, and logical. Today's libraries can provide support for any of those styles. Academic libraries in particular provide collections and services that support all these learning styles (Pashler, McDaniel, Rohrer, & Bjork, 2008).

Models of reading depict the relationship of the reader with the "text." Constructivist and connectionist elements mean that the reader brings context to reading. There is a feedback loop between the reader and the text. "Literacy" can mean the ability to read—to decode a text—but literacy is really multiple literacies, with linguistic and cultural aspects. Librarians are committed to creating users who are information literate, which is a complex aspect of literacy that includes the act of reading (Singer and Ruddell, 1985). Librarians must bear these in mind as they develop collections, programs, and services that will lead to student success.

Freire (1970) is a classic work that espouses the "liberatory" nature of education and an inclusive and dialogical model of pedagogy. Cain (2002) explores the role of reading in an electronic and digital culture, finding reading to persist as a private activity that leads to scholarship, and which should be encouraged by librarians. Trifonas (2000) uses a critical theory approach to propose a "revolutionary pedagogy" that challenges conventional forms of knowledge and of teaching. Morrell (2012) explores the meaning of literacy in the 21st century, defining it to include facility with digital technology as well as the ability to use and interpret information that is retrieved. Taylor (2008) discusses metaphors and discourses employed in a literacy course for adult learners, finding them infused with the values of those in authority. Rutten (2011) discusses narratives about literacy from the experience of college students who become part of the discourse community of higher education. Agnello (2008) examines educational policies for discourses of literacy and applying the findings in a classroom setting. Ajayi (2011) studies the use of video in a third-grade classroom to teach language arts through the use of social semiotics. Goodfellow (2011) explores the idea of digital literacy in higher education, including the idea that such literacies are "transformative" for higher education teaching. Pascarella (2008) speaks of the mere use of new media versus the idea of "critical digital literacy" that would improve the abstract notion of pedagogy through teacher and learner cognition and practice. Kellner (1998) discusses new literacies, including media, information, and technology literacy, including the idea that teachers learn from students and that education should be restructured to allow for pragmatic experimentation in a way that generally adheres to the principles of John Dewey.

Critical literacy and multiple literacies are important to an understanding of the educational environment, including higher education. Critical literacy explores the discourses of reading and of texts, and interrogates the power structures reflected there. These concepts are found in the work of Paolo Freire (1970) and others. Critical literacy and critical reading are part of a poststructuralist, postpositivist, and postmodern environment that includes a multicultural and relativist point of view.

The values of librarianship include the creation of an open environment of free thought and free inquiry. They include lifelong learning and autonomous reading and learning. Libraries guard the privacy of readers and do not pass judgment on opinions.

## 1.6  TEACHING, RESEARCH, AND PUBLIC SERVICE

The general goals of universities are teaching, research, and public service. Those goals are intertwined and inseparable. They support each other, and all have benefits for students, faculty, and the community. The current information environment has changed teaching, research, and service. It has changed students and faculty, and it has changed libraries and librarians. The powerful and rapidly changing information technology that is available to more and more people is changing the ways in which people teach, learn, communicate, read, write, shop, work, and so on. In particular, the world of Web 2.0 gives educators the opportunity to rethink and question every aspect of the teaching and learning process: semesters, credit hours, curricula, lectures, tests, term papers, all the things that have been the elements of higher education in particular for decades or even centuries. Libraries have the opportunity to rethink collections, programs, and services. What should we collect? How should we provide access? What forms of teaching and assistance should we provide? What impact will these activities have on the success of students?

The teaching role of the university is a means for scholars to impart knowledge to succeeding generations of young people and to adult learners. It is a varied and interactive process. Its methods differ among fields and disciplines. Teaching relies on written texts, scientific data, images, music, and other information formats. It relies on techniques such as lectures, discussions, group and individual assignments that involve an array of different activities, and on reading and writing. Libraries support the teaching process by providing all those formats of information and instruction on using them, by providing spaces for collaboration and individual work and study.

Research involves both faculty and students and takes many different forms, including the many methods of the humanities, social sciences, and sciences. Campuses provide laboratories, animals, farms, chemicals, engineering testing materials, materials for visual arts, recital halls and practice rooms, theaters, texts, and the technological infrastructure for experiments, surveys, the creation of content such as digital archives. Libraries support research by providing information resources of all kinds. These include journal literature, scholarly monographs, scores, sound and video recordings, and archival material that is unique and a primary source of research data.

Academic libraries support teaching and research, but their programs contribute to those missions as well. Reference and instruction provide interaction with faculty and students that teaches them to be information literate, including evaluating information. Catalogs and other finding aids create content and package information that is used in research and teaching. These programs support critical thinking and can foster a culture of reading and inquiry, which are clearly elements of student success.

In the past all library programs were delivered in person. Books and journals stood on a shelf, students and faculty visited the library to check out and use materials, and references and instruction were all delivered face to face. Today there are still print collections and in-person services, but collections and services are increasingly digital and virtual. In many ways, personal contact still drives digital and virtual communication just as it did print collections.

## 1.7 ACADEMIC LIBRARIES IN TRANSITION

Su (2006) reviews the literature on individual and organizational learning in academic libraries, libraries as learning organizations, and job-related learning. Fowler (1998) looks at organizational learning and innovation in university libraries at the individual, departmental, and organizational levels. McGuigan (2012) discusses the management of change in the context of organization theory and the role of organizational development in academic libraries. Giesecke and McNeil (2004) also review the concept of the learning organization, including steps to implement this model in an academic library.

Staley and Malenfant (2010) present 26 scenarios for the coming 15 years for academic libraries and their institutions, based on assessment of societal trends. The trends are weighed as to impact and probability and provide libraries with a way to create a new vision and reengineer their services. The Association of Research Libraries (ARL, 2012) addresses the role of collections in the academic library of the 21st century, urging libraries to be data and user driven in their approach.

Kelly and Kross (2002) look at the role of academic libraries in student retention, including diversity and information/technology literacy and partnerships with others on campus. Harris (2010) reports on efforts by an academic library to show leadership in student retention. Theories of retention include that of Tinto (2006), who emphasizes a model of social and academic integration, and Bean and Eaton's (2001) model, which looks at academic, sociopsychological, and environmental factors that affect retention—personal attention in reference and instruction builds student confidence. Tinto's model leads the library to provide study space, research assistance (including peer-to-peer assistance), and a common learning environment.

"Libraries of the Future" is a project of the British Library, JISC, the Research Information Network (RIN), Research Libraries UK (RLUK) and the Society of College, National and University Libraries (SCONUL). It created three scenarios for the libraries of 2050, using two axes: open/closed and state/market. The three scenarios are Wild West, Beehive, and Walled Garden. The scenarios can be used in planning and strategizing.

The ACRL Research Planning and Review Committee (2012) discuss the top 10 trends affecting academic libraries, including communicating and proving their own value, data curation, digital preservation, the general environment of higher education, the continuing importance of information technology, the emergence of mobile computing, patron-driven acquisition (especially of ebooks), the library's role in scholarly communication, approaches to staffing, and the demands and behavior of users.

## 1.8  STRATEGIES FOR ACADEMIC LIBRARIES

Given this environment, what are the best strategies for academic libraries to create and manage a culture that promotes reading, learning, and public service, and contributes to student success? There are a number of ways to do this.

The first is in the approach to collections, which remain a central aspect of library services. Academic libraries must continue to provide access to resources in all formats and examine the persistent privileging of text over audio, video, etc. Likewise, it is important to continue working on creating a usable and consistent interface in the library catalog and other databases and discovery tools that will encourage students to use library resources rather than rely exclusively on open access Web resources.

Academic libraries can be leaders in student success by designing programs and services that meet the needs of students with different learning styles, and by helping students learn to evaluate information sources. Libraries should continue to embrace technology and show how that technology can be used to consume, interpret, and build on scholarly and research material.

The roles of librarians include teacher, expert, systematizer, problem-solver, and scholar. All of these roles can contribute to student success. Academic librarians can create opportunities to interact with students as individuals or in groups. They can deliver instruction in a number of modes. Librarians have a vital role in teaching critical thinking and in teaching students to be independent researchers.

There is a lively conversation taking place on college and university campuses about the elements of student success. Libraries are a vital part of that conversation and must continue to be leaders in this process, partnering with writing centers, academic departments, honors programs, and many others to provide support for student success.

A crucial part of the campus conversation on student success is the consideration of space. Libraries have dedicated physical spaces, and the "library as place" has been an issue since the dawn of the digital age. While users can happily and successfully access and use information resources from anywhere at any time, there is a resurgence in the discussions of library spaces, not just as places for individual and group study, but as shared spaces for other campus units and activities.

The administration, management, and organization of the library are essential to accomplishing these goals. The library must value learning in a way that allows its employees to learn and explore in everything they do. The idea of the learning organization is explored in Chapter 2, "Managing the Impact of Scholarly Publications," and that model or a similar one is important in creating a library that moves, changes, and responds, while at the same time preserving the freedom to learn and the freedom to teach for librarians and library users.

# CHAPTER 2

# Managing the Impact of Scholarly Publications

## 2.1 INTRODUCTION

In order to deliver relevance, value, and impact to customers, academic library managers work from an assessment framework and an "organic" thinking approach, which puts people before resources. This is known as a "disaggregated model" and is part of the online teaching milieu, in which almost half of faculty are adjunct instructors. The role of the research library in scholarly communication addresses two variables: the explosion of printed materials and their concomitant increase in the price as well as the labor to catalog them. This jeopardizes the library's ability to create and maintain the collections for remote users. The emergence of electronic information technologies that have made it possible to use entirely new methods of organizing services and collections must be responsive, even if students are not taking advantage of them. Research libraries' percentage of the university budget has shrunk; serial prices have continued to rise exponentially, and salaries as well as employment prospects have all declined. In the midst of these problems, digital technologies, combined with library expertise in information management and bibliographic control, access, dissemination, and preservation, have provided new opportunities for access and for academic librarians to play a more active role in the publication of scholarly information. In the last decade, initiatives in North American academic libraries have revolved around electronic presses in their own institutions, and the use of WorldCat to locate books, articles, and media that are held by the parent institution and other institutions.

*Managing Academic Libraries*
ISBN 978-1-84334-621-0
http://dx.doi.org/10.1016/B978-1-84334-621-0.00002-9

## 2.2 ECONOMICS AND TECHNOLOGY

Conventional print journals bring in total revenues to publishers of about $4000 per article. However, there are many flourishing electronic journals that operate without money changing hands. Although it is questionable whether this model can satisfy scholars' needs, the quality is adequate for most readers, and costs can be recovered through subscription fees or charges to authors (Odlyzko, 1997).

Journal subscription costs are only one part of the scholarly information system. Internal operating costs of research libraries are at least twice as high as their acquisition budgets. Thus for every article that brings in $4000 in revenues to publishers, libraries in aggregate spend $8000 on ordering, cataloging, shelving, checking out materials, and reference help. The scholarly journal crisis is clearly a library cost crisis. If publishers suddenly started to give away their print material for free, the growth of the literature would in a few years bring us back to a crisis situation that we are experiencing today (Odlyzko, 1). At one time, library Website usability testing was seen as a powerful indicator of design problems and would help to clarify information-seeking needs. However, in the article "Broccoli Librarianship and Google-Bred Patrons, or What's Wrong with Usability Testing?" Debbie Vaughn and Burton Callicott (2003) wrote that the testing instrument reflected the librarians' interpretation of a useful (or good-for-you vegetable) Website, rather than what patrons accustomed to Google and other search engines wanted, that is, simplicity and ease of use. The "library faith" theory of helping patrons is not realistic. The authors stated, "effective usability testing requires that participants possess a basic understanding of scholarly research, library language, and the functions of a library Website. In addition, testing instruments should be carefully constructed to account for usefulness, not just ease of use. Unless these conditions are met, usability testing will be misleading, ineffectual, and counterproductive" (p. 1). Collection management in the future will focus on preserving and cataloguing social networking sites and other emerging digital forms.

## 2.3  MORE ECONOMICS AND TECHNOLOGY

Conventional print journals bring in total revenues to publishers of about $4000 per article. However, there are many flourishing electronic journals that operate without money changing hands. Although it is questionable whether this model can satisfy scholars' needs, the quality is adequate for most readers, and costs can be recovered through subscription fees or charges to authors (Odlyzko, 1997).

Journal subscription costs are only one part of the scholarly information system. Internal operating costs of research libraries are at least twice as high as their acquisition budgets. Thus for every article that brings in $4000 in revenues to publishers, libraries in aggregate spend $8000 on ordering, cataloging, shelving, and checking out material and reference help. The scholarly journal crisis is clearly a library cost crisis. Odlyzko wrote that if publishers suddenly started to give away their print material for free, the growth of the literature would in a few years bring us back to a crisis situation we are experiencing today. (Odlyzko, 1). Published literature may become a smaller portion of collection programs in academic libraries as the focus has shifted to preserving, cataloguing and curating emerging digital forms.

# CHAPTER 3

# Library and Information Science as a Discipline

## 3.1 INTRODUCTION

Library and information science (LIS) is highly interdisciplinary by nature and has been affected by the evolution of technologies (Prebor, 2010; Saracevic, 1999; Tang, 2004). Bates (2005, p. 12) declares that the main purpose of LIS is to provide access to "meaningful recorded information through variety of channels." In order to provide such access, it is necessary to know what information is needed, how such information is sought, evaluated, and used to meet these needs, and so on.

LIS as a discipline has a particular focus on providing information to end users (Missingham, 2006; Um & Feather, 2007) and the functions of the information professional are determined by the needs of users that they serve. Hence, the information profession is "greatly and properly influenced by social, cultural and political factors out with the immediate domain of the profession" (Um & Feather, 2007, p. 264). Rapid changes in the social and economic environment have influenced the scope and organization of library and information services and, therefore, the library and information professions as well (Sacchanand, 2000). LIS is defined as making people informed through intermediation between inquirers and instrumented records.

Fourie (2004) believes that academic courses in LIS should be oriented toward "the development of survival and affective skills." Missingham (2006) suggests that practices and procedures in LIS education should meet the needs of the actual working environment. For example, instead of identifying the source of information and getting access to documents, they should evaluate, filter, extract, analyze, summarize, synthesize, and package information in a form that clients can use to make decisions (Khoo, 2005). However, information professionals should move from information work to knowledge work as users are looking for knowledge rather than just information.

*Managing Academic Libraries*
ISBN 978-1-84334-621-0
http://dx.doi.org/10.1016/B978-1-84334-621-0.00003-0

Gerolimos and Konsta (2008, p. 695) state that the LIS educated must be able to "recognize informational needs, manage users and encourage people with different skills to work." Library and information science is needed to develop problem-solving and decision making in the workplace for professional practitioners and also to provide optimal information services to researchers in other fields (Juznic & Urbanija, 2003).

Gerolimos (2009) identifies the qualifications and skills that LIS students should have when they graduate. He discovered that most library schools (49 LIS schools were examined from the United States, the United Kingdom, and Canada in May 2008) consider traditional librarianship a very important element. "Terms such as knowledge management and information literacy are not documented as qualifications but rather, as more generic fields of practice and knowledge for a librarian" (Gerolimos, 2009). According to Virkus (2003, p. 68) "being information literate is a necessity for information professionals because it helps them maintain a lifelong learning attitude that keeps them abreast of an ever changing information environment, while at the same time it enables them to develop as facilitators of learning to help users become information literate." She highlights the key characteristics of LIS students as follows:

- Be able to recognize when he/she needs information
- Be aware of what different channels and sources are available
- Be able to evaluate information effectively
- Be able to manage and apply information
- Be able to synthesize information and use it to create new knowledge and understanding
- Be aware of the cultural, ethical, economic, legal, and social issues surrounding the use of information (Virkus, 2003, p. 71).

LIS professionals support a wide variety of users in their access to information to develop necessary practical skills and techniques needed for the better utilization of information. This is particularly so because of the distinguishing characteristics of the LIS discipline and its user-oriented features that LIS professionals apply to facilitate users. However, the core mission of LIS is to develop information professionals who are able to educate users' information needs in the following areas:

- Diagnose users' information needs
- Respond to the users' information needs
- Educate users how to find, evaluate, and use information

In order to gain an understanding of the contribution of the LIS discipline to the development of information professionals, the information literacy (IL) competencies listed following are discussed from an LIS view in relation to the LIS core areas of curriculum as described previously.

### 3.1.1 Determining Information Needs

One of the major concerns of LIS professionals is to determine the information needs of users through courses such as "collection development," "organizing," and "reference services." Belkin (1997) considers LIS professionals as facilitators of the effective communication of desired information between "human generator and human user." LIS professionals support a wide variety of uses, from retrieving information, to organizing and simplifying massive datasets (Jin & Bouthillier, 2012). Indeed, in the LIS literature, LIS has been seen to employ a wide variety of methods to help users of information skills to access the available knowledge, and because of that LIS tends to be defined as a profession whose main concern is to deal with information needs of their users (Juznic & Urbanija, 2003).

*The information professions comprise all those persons directly engaged in design, management and delivery of information, information collections and information services to the communities of users.*

*Carr (2003)*

### 3.1.2 Locating Information

As can be conceived from the descriptions of LIS, one of the key characteristics of information professionals (IPs) is to support users in finding information (Fisher, 2004). Locating information is an important core of the LIS discipline. According to Virkus (2003), libraries and IPs help people to access information and satisfy their information needs. It should be included in any LIS course such as cataloguing, indexing, and reference services and sources at any level (Parirokh, 2008). The LIS Education project in Europe analyzed 10 curricular themes within the LIS curricula in Europe and found that information seeking and information retrieval are the core subject areas in the LIS school curricula (Borup Larsen, Kajberg, & Lørring, 2005). Indeed, Gorman (2003) at the joint EUCLID/ALISE conference, devised a core curriculum of LIS that is applicable to all schools. He found that selecting and finding information in all forms is one of the areas in which information professionals should be knowledgeable. Juznic and Urbanija (2003) highlight that LIS professionals are usually involved in the process of retrieving information. Wittwer (2001) declares that the LIS educated should be competent in searching for and locating information.

Referring to these statements, locating information in the LIS discipline is an important skill, the lack of which may cause frustrations in using information and can reduce the performance of information professionals in serving users.

### 3.1.3 Evaluating Information

Indeed, "Evaluating information resources have always been part of the remit of IPs. However the knowledge of evaluative techniques is all the more important for IPs" (Ashcroft, 2004, p. 84). Ashcroft believes that the LIS educated must have evaluation skills, particularly in the current changing environment. Indeed, in the LIS context, analysis and synthesis are the main activities. Classification, abstracting, collecting, and subject indexing are considered as these main activities. The important element of classification, abstracting, and indexing processes is to understand the content; obviously, they are also considered evaluating and critical reading activities. Critical reading includes the following (Koltay, 2007):

• Determining the purpose of the text and assessing how the central claims are developed,
• Making judgments about the intended audience of the text,
• Distinguishing the different kinds of reasoning in the text,
• Examining the evidence and sources of the writing.

It is clear from what has been discussed thus far that critical reading is closely connected to the LIS program and includes the abilities and the activities of reading and writing.

### 3.1.4  Using Information Ethically

Likewise, using information ethically is necessary in the field of library and information studies. The contributions that library and information studies can make to knowledge can be significant by paying due attention to information ethics. It should be one of the important aspects of education in library and information studies. According to Jin and Bouthillier (2012):

> *This profession greatly values and adheres to ethical principles on information seeking, gathering, organizing, and disseminating. For example, in the ALA Code of Ethics (American Library Association (ALA, 2008)), it is articulated that information professionals protect each information user's right to privacy and confidentiality with respect to information sought or received and resources consulted, borrowed, acquired or transmitted.*
>
> **Jin and Bouthillier (2012, p. 143)**

Hence, we may say that LIS concentrates on using information ethically.

### 3.1.5  Using Information for Specific Purpose

Hjørland (2000, p. 520) describes library and information science as "a knowledge producing field and a knowledge utilizing field." Although only a minor amount of the knowledge is produced by LIS professionals, some types of knowledge are often taught at LIS schools. Some examples are:

- Broad cultural knowledge;
- Knowledge about the different domains communicated/promoted (eg, music, law, medicine);
- Knowledge about the philosophy and sociology of science;
- Economic and administrative knowledge;
- Knowledge about specific information sources, such as databases, Internet resources, etc.;
- Knowledge about information technology (IT);
- Language and communication skills and much more. (Hjørland, 2000, p. 502)

Most IPs follow a simple three-step methodology to handle information: seeking for and receiving information, analyzing and synthesizing information into an organized one, and empowering the user to respond to an information need. The point of departure is that "in most cases the final goal of library activities is generating texts" (Horváth, 1999). This is why LIS uses text not only to analyze but also to produce knowledge.

## 3.2 INFORMATION LITERACY IN LIS DISCIPLINE

The focus of IL education, which is to find, access, evaluate information, and use the information for specific purposes, is quite different from the focus of LIS programs in general. While there are courses in most LIS programs on "information sources and services" and "reference services and information retrieval," they focus more on the application aspects of information. Drawing on the literature on IL in the LIS discipline, approaches to adapt IL to the LIS discipline tend to integrate IL into the curriculum as a part of a class that focuses on teaching IL—through a separate class or as an approach to learning. The idea of learning through involving with information has been presented in the literature. It is worth noting that IL skills have been identified as a way of "engaging with information and learning about the subject" (Bruce & Candy, 2000), and also "a way of learning" (Kuhlthau, 1993). At the same time, "acquiring information is a type of learning, using information is also another type of learning" (Lupton, 2008). Therefore, as illustrated in Fig. 3.1, information can emerge from learning, while learning can generate from using information.

In particular, the relationship between engaging with information, using, and learning was identified by Lupton (2008). He categorized the relationship between IL and learning as a cyclic action of learning in music composition:

1. Creating a composition through applying the techniques of composition. In this way, students acquire the techniques (information) and apply them (using information and then learning).

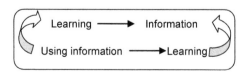

**Figure 3.1** Using information approach.

2. Applying techniques (using information, which is followed by learning) and then learning from the information that was generated through the process.

3. Experiencing learning through creating a composition that is somehow expressing oneself. This involves a process of "using information as a form of learning and then learning as a form of using information" (Lupton, 2008).

Therefore, it could be argued that IL and learning are two sides of the same coin.

IL could not be just a set of skills as it involves understanding the ways that information flows in the system of thought. In other words, students should identify and be engaged with a significant problem rather than focus on acquiring knowledge (Elmborg, 2006). In this way, they learn how to control their lives as active agents to find the answer to the questions that matter to them and the people around them (Elmborg, 2006). This view depicts the critical role of IL to "learn how to learn," which is essential for effective "lifelong learning."

Contemporary with the emergence of the new information environments, tools, and technologies, IL has been highlighted as a necessity for IPs (Campello & Abreu, 2005; Johnston & Webber, 2004; Andretta, cited in Virkus, 2003). Varalakskhmi (2009) points out that:

> The primary task of information professional[s] is to enhance the information literacy among the users of an organization. At present users may have basic knowledge in searching for information, but there is a need for teaching and training them in the advanced and more advanced searching. Information literacy will provide the user the ability to acquire and interpret information, to manage information, to communicate information, and to apply information for specific task.
>
> **Varalakskhmi (2009, p. 79)**

To make IPs information literate, they have to be fully aware of the importance of IL as a concept, understand its relevance in contemporary societies, and learn about main aspects of teaching IL (Hebrang Grgić & Špiranec, 2013). Indeed, there is a trend to help them maintain a lifelong learning attitude so that they are able to adapt with the changing information environment and also help users to become information literate (Foster, 2006; Virkus, 2003). The following approaches are characteristic of this view:

- Make them aware of information literacy as a concept;
- To become information literate themselves;
- Learn about key aspects of teaching information literacy.

These approaches imply that the components of IL need to be embedded in LIS education in order to develop lifelong learners; however, there is no clear approach in this regard. Virkus (2003), for example, although she acknowledges the importance of IL in LIS discipline, does not deliver a guideline for teaching and embedding IL to facilitate and develop students' learning in a way that they can learn how to learn. In this regard, she stresses that LIS students need to understand IL holistically. She argues that IL as a base of lifelong learning could be a necessary component of LIS discipline. This is because of the focus of LIS in user education; it demands lifelong learners to facilitate others.

In the following section, the interconnection between LIS and IL is discussed.

## 3.3  RELATIONSHIPS BETWEEN LIS AND IL

If it is expected to integrate IL into LIS curricula, first there should be a clear understanding of how these two domains relate to each other. Information literacy is often discussed in all phases and all subject areas during the whole education process (Boekhorst, 2003). Although there are different ways to conceptualize information literacy, they can be divided into five categories:

1. Recognizing a need for information;
2. Finding the needed information;
3. Evaluating the information found;
4. Using information ethically;
5. Using information effectively to address the specific problem (ACRL, 2000a; ALA, 2000; CILIP, 2006; UNESCO, 2005).

The horizons of LIS have enlarged considerably since the appearance of the Internet (Jin & Bouthillier, 2012), but the core skills of information professions are still relevant in the age of electronic information provision (Sharp, 2001). Sharp argues that the skills such as cataloguing, classification, indexing, and enquiry work and user education all still have a place and are applicable in facilitating effective Internet use.

IPs are facing some challenges, but they should be able to adapt their existing skills, which call for traditional librarianship skills such as evaluating, cataloguing, and analyzing information and being flexible within a changing work environment (Ashcroft, 2004; Bierman, 2000; Goulding, 2001; Pedley, 2001; Sharp, 2001). There is not much literature that specifically addresses the link between LIS and IL. It requires that LIS and IL have a complementary relation. While LIS focuses on how to retrieve, organize, and simplify massive datasets (Jin & Bouthillier, 2012), IL emphasizes "learn how to learn." The concept of LIS focuses on the physical arrangement of information, to learn to access and use information sources (Foster, 2006). In addition, LIS concentrates more on the format and properties of information, and IL focuses on the content of information to solve a problem. However, the knowledge and skills of LIS professionals on seeking and evaluating information may play a very active role in the IL field. Where LIS uses information from stable resources with structured form, IL copes with information from structured and unstructured forms. Due to a complementary relation, IL can play an active role to expand LIS into nontraditional areas, but it cannot be considered as the foundations of information literacy because when "one has no access to libraries or text, information literacy may not only be an unattainable goal, it may be deemed irrelevant at this time" (Moore, 2002).

Hence, we may say that LIS can serve as an introduction to IL and IL completes LIS in a way of information use. IL should be treated as a new lens of traditional LIS because core IL skills would be essential for future information professionals. Therefore, LIS and IL could have an interactive relationship if they come together well.

The features and characteristics listed in Table 3.1 depict the LIS discipline as a novel area to develop information literate librarians and IPs. This study will contribute toward the development of information literate librarians and IPs into the LIS discipline.

**Table 3.1** Characteristics of LIS in Comparison with IL Competencies

| Information literacy competencies | Library and Information Science |
|---|---|
| Determining information needs | Main concern of LIS is to deal with information needs of their users (Carr, 2003; Gerolimos & Konsta, 2008; Jin & Bouthillier, 2012; Juznic & Urbanija, 2003) |
| Locating information | Focus of LIS is in finding information (Borup Larsen, Kajberg, & Lørring, 2005; Fisher, 2004; Gorman, 2003; Juznic & Urbanija, 2003; Virkus, 2003; Wittwer, 2001) |
| Evaluating information | The important element of classification, abstracting, and indexing process is to understand the content; obviously they are evaluating activity (Jin & Bouthillier, 2012; Koltay, 2007) |
| Using information ethically | Information ethics, copyrights, and licenses are important aspects of education and practice in library and information science (ALA, 2008; Wu & Chiu, 2011) |
| Using information for specific purpose | LIS is a knowledge-producing field (Hjørland, 2000) |

# CHAPTER 4

# Managing Higher-Order Thinking Skills

## 4.1 INTRODUCTION

Librarians have been criticized for being merely practitioners with no basis in theory, evidence, or data for the decisions that are made about library programs and services. Several things are helping to change this situation. One factor is the demand for accountability being felt by colleges and universities, which has created a more data-driven environment. Another is the ready availability of data (more difficult to obtain in the past). For example, libraries now have access to usage statistics about the collection that were previously difficult to procure and compile. Spreadsheets and other software allow easy manipulation of data, including budget data for projections and scenario building. Moreover, academic librarians are becoming more scholarly, more comfortable with qualitative and quantitative data, as well as more user oriented as a part of being accountable. This environment of analysis and assessment is one in which higher–order thinking skills are essential, and are an essential element of management and administration.

Higher-order thinking skills are those in the three highest levels of Bloom's taxonomy. The taxonomy was created in 1956 and is a classification of the objectives of education. The levels include knowledge, comprehension, application, analysis, synthesis, and evaluation, with the last three being the higher-order skills. Bloom separates learning into three domains: cognitive, affective, and psychomotor, ie, knowing, feeling, and doing. Bloom's taxonomy provides a framework for encouraging higher-order thinking in library users, particularly as part of information literacy programs, in which critical thinking is an essential component of instruction. Higher-order thinking is also crucial in the actions of librarians and library staff.

*Managing Academic Libraries*
ISBN 978-1-84334-621-0
http://dx.doi.org/10.1016/B978-1-84334-621-0.00004-2

29

The elements of higher-order thinking in library administration and library operations include critical thinking, but also spatial and mathematical reasoning, multiple literacies including computer literacy and the ability to gather and manipulate data. Emotional intelligence is part of "affective" learning and is an important element in library administration. This chapter presents the use of higher-order thinking skills in programs for library users, such as information literacy, and also in the management of library programs and services.

Since libraries are learning organizations, it is reasonable to think that they are also organizations that value and practice higher-order thinking skills, including critical thinking. Academic libraries have instruction programs that teach information literacy. Information literacy is closely related to critical thinking, and information literacy programs try to teach students to approach information resources critically. Beyond these instruction programs, however, libraries need all employees to acquire and use higher-order thinking skills to plan and carry out programs and services, to handle budgets, hire and supervise, work with faculty and administrators on campus, and so on.

Line (2005) is critical of librarians' reaction, or lack of it, to the rapidly changing social and educational environment. Hazen (2011) sees this inability to understand and react as a product of a lack of a community of practice and social inclusiveness. He recommends finding appropriate partners for collaboration and then assessing programs and communicating their value.

Academic librarians help develop higher-order thinking skills in university students because their mission statement is to organize the resources for inquiry-based learning. Information literacy is a central concept of academic librarianship and higher-order thinking skills are at the core of information literacy. Teaching faculty can help integrate information literacy skills into the curriculum. Saunders (2009) found support for moving from a focus on information retrieval skills to the more complex, transferable areas of information literacy. The move from bibliographic instruction to information literacy is a complicated transition. Foo et al. (2002) observe that librarians' strong foundation in information needs and information-seeking behavior can be broadened to include other research skills.

Higher-order thinking skills in students are obviously connected to academic success. Noncognitive, psychosocial variables are also factors in success and librarians must be aware of these, including things like gender and race. Understanding noncognitive factors of performance require what Montiel-Overall (2009) calls "cultural competence." She states further that "there is a critical need to develop cultural competence among LIS professionals to address social, linguistic, and academic needs of culturally diverse individuals who represent a population most in need of library services" (199). Montiel-Overall identifies three domains in which cultural competence is developed: cognitive, interpersonal, and environmental. Managing higher-order thinking skills as part of information literacy instruction requires paying attention to differences. The National Committee of Inquiry into Higher Education Summary Report (1997) emphasizes support for lifelong learning. Cooke et al. (2011) evaluated the impact of academic liaison librarians on their user communities. The authors found that faculty were not aware of the many skills that the librarians possessed, including in-depth subject knowledge, IT skills, and communication skills.

## 4.2 INFORMATION LITERACY

Information literacy is the foundation of lifelong learning. Information literacy helps people use and understand multiple literacies, and contributes to cultural competence and the use of higher-order thinking skills. One important higher-order thinking skill is evaluation. Information literacy includes the ability to select the most appropriate information from the vast amount that is available. Mac-Donald (2004) emphasizes the role librarians have in choosing and evaluating information.

There is a great deal of literature on information literacy and on the importance of higher-order thinking skills. Krathwohl (2002) discusses the revision of Bloom's taxonomy, including differences between the original and revised versions. Mayer (2002) describes new psychological research that serves as an updated guide to the use of Bloom's taxonomy. Hills (2004) explores quality in education, including the use of Bloom's taxonomy and its use in college writing and literacy tutoring. Zohar and Dori (2003) look at research that shows that both high- and low-achieving students can benefit from being taught to use higher order thinking skills. Brierton (2012) discusses research that demonstrates employers' need for workers who have higher-order thinking skills and are therefore flexible and able to learn new things quickly. The author explores the development of these skills through the use of synchronous and asynchronous discussion boards. Asynchronous discussion provides more opportunity for reflection and was found to be more useful in developing higher-level skills. Williams (2003) "presents a framework of the five R's: relevance, richness, relatedness, rigor, and recursiveness." This framework can be used in K–12 instruction to encourage critical and creative thinking. Marlow and Inman (1992) look at the perceptions of teachers regarding higher-order thinking skills, using a pre- and post-test during "a workshop emphasizing active involvement in developing and using activities to encourage improvement and expansion of thinking skills in children." Cousins and Ross (1993) explore using computers to improve correlational reasoning, including comparing task-based and general software and looking at students' background and attitudes. Berger (2006) discusses new media literacies, which include "Distributed Cognition—the ability to interact meaningfully with tools that expand mental capacities." Anderson (2005) describes the revision of Bloom's taxonomy by eight educators from 1995 to 2000. They produced the "Taxonomy Table," with categories: Remember, Understand, Apply, Analyze, Evaluate, and Create, and the four types of knowledge: Factual, Conceptual, Procedural, and Metacognitive.

A number of authors explore of higher-order thinking skills in various academic disciplines. Sheldon (2005) looks for higher-order thinking skills among students of music education, finding that the curriculum can be successful in inculcating these skills. Narayanan and Adithan (2012) investigate the use of Bloom's taxonomy to foster higher-order thinking in engineering students. Steer and McConnell (2008) examine undergraduate courses in geology as a way to teach higher-order thinking skills, including "quantitative skills, developing a conceptual understanding and using scientific principles, and increasing the ability to think critically." Oliver and Dobele (2007) explore the use of Bloom's taxonomy in the cognitive aspect of assessment tasks in first-year computer science tasks, including designing courses with a "Bloom rating." Fletcher, Flahive, Ford, and Fletcher (2010) look at physical geology textbooks and the need to integrate critical thinking and other higher-order thinking skills, including Bloom's taxonomy. There were four strategies for integration: inclusion of learning objectives, testing of "knowledge, comprehension, and analysis," organization of chapters into two-page sections with queries at the end of each, and use of artwork that accompanies questions based on all six levels of Bloom's taxonomy. Madhuri, Kantamreddi, and Prakash Goteti (2012) describe research in a first-year chemical engineering course that explored the role of active learning in encouraging higher-order thinking.

Teachers in primary, secondary, and higher education settings have created curricula that emphasize higher-order thinking. Ma (2009) found a positive correlation between the quality of the collaborative learning process and the level of cognitive skills employed. Ying Chau (2006) describes a tutorial designed to foster higher-order thinking through the use of multiple learning styles and multiple intelligences. Polly (2011) looks at the overlap between higher-order thinking skills and "a set of knowledge components referred to as Technological, Pedagogical, and Content Knowledge (TPACK)." Torff (2003) studies teachers' use of higher-order thinking skills, finding that more-experienced teachers depended less on curricular content and more on higher-order thinking skills. Thomas, Davis, and Kazlauskas (2007) advocate the use of "scaffolding" to develop critical thinking and metacognitive skills. Nichols (2010) focuses on higher-order thinking skills in distance education and the need to incorporate activities that build and assess these skills.

Academic librarians have a strong role in collaborating with faculty on information literacy and higher-order thinking. Ellis and Whatley (2008) explore research by undergraduates and the need for librarians to support the skills needed for this research by providing instruction in critical thinking as part of information literacy instruction. Bodi (1988) looks at bibliographic or library instruction as a way to encourage critical thinking. Dintrone (1989) discusses critical thinking and library instruction, including K–12 and higher education. Whitmire (1998) explored the development of critical thinking skills in undergraduates. Factors leading to success include "focused academic library activities" as well as interaction with faculty and active learning activities. Rao, Cameron, and Gaskin-Noel (2009) discuss online information literacy courses and the redesign of one course to incorporate "critical thinking, information literacy, critical reading, quantitative reasoning, and writing." Taylor (2008) investigates using library instruction to teach critical thinking, using a vocabulary-building activity with business students. Samson (2010) used the ACRL information literacy competency standards to assess information literacy in first-year and capstone students. The findings indicated significant differences between the two groups. Weiner (2011) explores the similarities and differences between critical thinking and information literacy. Weiner did a content analysis of literature from education, library science, and health science, finding that information literacy was involved with all Bloom's cognitive functions. This finding suggests that information literacy instruction could be powerful in teaching the concepts in Bloom's taxonomy and improving higher-order thinking skills. Johnson, Lindsay, and Walter (2008) also explored the relationship between critical thinking and information literacy. Librarians participated in a first-year experience program that encouraged critical thinking, resulting in more involvement on campus for library information literacy efforts. Gilbert (2009) describes a pilot program to "measure the effects of a multiple library instruction session module on students' research skills in the first semester." The results showed that students who had received this instruction had greater confidence and greater use of library resources. Aydelott (2007) discusses the construction of an interactive information literacy tutorial that was based on ACRL's Information Literacy Competency Standards for Science and Engineering/Technology. The tutorial includes critical thinking and can be used as part of a for-credit course and as a standalone resource. Mathson and Lorenzen (2008) describe an information literacy course taught by librarians, which incorporates critical thinking skills. The course is a one-credit, eight-week course that teaches evaluation of Website authority and reliability. The success of the course has been measured with pre- and posttest self-assessments by students. Oakleaf (2009) presents the "Information Literacy Instruction Assessment Cycle (ILIAC)," which "encourages librarians to articulate learning outcomes clearly, analyze them meaningfully, celebrate learning achievements, and diagnose problem areas."

Assessment is an essential part of the culture of accountability and crucial to information literacy instruction. Benjamin (2008) advises higher education institutions to conduct assessments of higher-order thinking skills as the "key aims of instruction" as a way to develop effective pedagogy. Milner-Bolotin and Nashon (2012) discuss visual-spatial literacy and its relationship to higher-order thinking skills. They describe instruction in visual-spatial literacy in the biology curriculum as a way of promoting higher-order thinking skills. Pena and Almaguer (2012) describe the use of a rubric that evaluated higher-order thinking in assessing written reflections on learning theory by first-semester teacher education students. Most students reached a level of four "on a scale of 1–6 with 1 being recall and 6 being synthesis." Hopson, Simms, and Knezek (2001) found that a technology-rich classroom had a beneficial effect on the development of higher-order thinking skills in fifth-grade students.

Menchaca (2012) explores the relationship between social networking and learning, including the "consequences of personalization associated with such tools on research, critical thinking, and information literacy." Kirton, Barham, and Brady (2008) report on research on the use of critical thinking skills in information literacy instruction in academic and government libraries.

## 4.3  CRITICAL THINKING IN LIBRARY ORGANIZATIONS

While information literacy instruction is a core service that includes instruction in higher-order thinking skills, these skills are clearly essential as an aspect of library administration and management. Glynn (2006) describes the use of evidence-based librarianship (EBL) and one of its most important aspects, "critical appraisal." EBL can be a tool in research design but also an approach to critical thinking and higher-order thinking within the library organization. Somerville and Brar (2009) used EBL to reengineer user experience in an academic library. This was a collaborative activity among librarians, teaching faculty, and students. Promís (2008) looks at emotional intelligence in academic librarians, examining job advertisements for "soft skills" that include many higher-order thinking skills. Booth (2006) looks at EBL and its origins in evidence-based practice in health care. The author proposes a conceptual framework for asking questions leading to EBL. The "SPICE" model asks, "Setting – where? Perspective – for whom? Intervention – what? Comparison – compared with what? Evaluation – with what result?" Greenwood and Cleeve (2008) propose an EBL model for public libraries. The authors see this approach as a way to use data in planning and decision-making process, which requires staff to acquire the skills to gather and interpret data. Eldredge (2006) describes the EBL approach and its origins in health sciences and health sciences librarianship, including "formulating answerable questions" and collecting data to answer them. Baker (2006) describes a study in which academic librarians used EBL to improve their information literacy program for freshmen, looking at it over an eight-year period. Blake and Ballance (2013) describe a seminar in evidence-based practice collaboratively designed by librarians and nurses, emphasizing "analysis of the literature, institutional models of practice change, and the importance of patient roles in guideline development." Bayley, Ferrell, and Mckinnell (2009) discuss a review of library operations done at McMaster University, the "birthplace of evidence-based practice." The review of operations was a step toward implementing EBL. Given (2006) discusses the role of qualitative research in EBL. Qualitative research provides important data that is just as essential as quantitative information. Koufogiannakis and Crumley (2006) look at the use of research to aid decision-making in libraries, including the general need "to establish a solid evidence base within our profession."

Perrault and Dixon (2007) describe a collection assessment effort that collected data to be used to improve library programs and services. Cody (2006) explores the difference between acquiring information and processing that information. The author emphasizes the need for librarians to add context to the information, an aspect of critical thinking. Gannon–Leary (2006) describes the UK initiative "Framework for MultiAgency Environments (FAME)" focusing on how "professionals and practitioners ... accessed and used information" and finding a need for more IT skills. Moreillon, Luhtala, and Russo (2011) look at resources for encouraging critical thinking and other higher-order thinking skills that are provided for teachers by the school library in a high school. Moran (2008) speaks to the need for systems thinking rather than "straight line thinking" in library planning and problem-solving.

Rahimi and Damirchi (2011) discuss Gardner's theory of multiple intelligences, which includes "linguistic intelligence, logical intelligence, spatial intelligence, bodily intelligence, musical intelligence, interpersonal intelligence, intrapersonal intelligence and naturalistic intelligence." Rahimi and Damirchi look at the relationship to critical thinking in an academic library.

Miller (2011) discusses the idea of "intelligent libraries," achieved through the use of higher-order thinking skills, multiple intelligences, and other similar models. Porter (2010) discusses the use of emotional intelligence in library administration. The author describes the role of emotional intelligence in "communication, trust, interpersonal relations, and crisis management." Smith (2006) uses the idea of multiple intelligences to explore the problems faced by people of different cultural backgrounds when accessing digital library resources. Hernon and Rossiter (2006) define emotional intelligence, which includes "self-management and managing relationships with others" and discuss its use and value in leadership. Kreitz (2009) investigates emotional intelligence as a characteristic of library directors and senior managers at members of the Association of Research Libraries (ARL) in the Western United States.

## 4.4  HIGHER-ORDER THINKING SKILLS IN ACADEMIC LIBRARIES

As the preceding review of recent research demonstrates, higher education in general, and academic libraries in particular, are deeply interested and deeply involved in teaching students to use higher-order thinking skills as the road to lifelong learning. At their most effective, they are also using these higher-order skills as the foundation for creating and assessing programs and services that help carry out the institutional mission. What must managers do to create continuing success in these areas?

As with the learning organization, the first step is to create a shared understanding of the significance of higher-order thinking skills. This requires managers to encourage and reward independent thought, open discussion, and dissent. To support a lively intellectual environment, it is also necessary to provide the education and training necessary to formulate questions and then gather and interpret data to provide answers to those questions. Librarians and library staff must have appropriate expertise in qualitative and quantitative research methods, which will allow them to be comfortable with data-driven decision-making.

Higher-order thinking skills demand an organization that embraces diversity. That diversity should include things like gender and ethnicity as well as diversity of thought, strengths, learning styles, and intelligences. In addition to employees strong in mathematical reasoning, verbal skills, and analytical ability, academic libraries should prize emotional intelligence and the cultural competence it implies.

The use of higher-order thinking skills, multiple intelligences, and cultural competency can be a foundation for EBL, a data-driven culture of assessment that creates library programs based on information based on user needs and behaviors. That approach is valid for every area of the library:

- Library administration sets the tone for the EBL environment by gathering and using data, and interpreting it with wisdom and expertise in the decision-making process. Statistics and other data from all library services is obviously useful to library administrators. That includes usage data, as well as human resources information, and data on funding, budgets, and expenditures. Administrators also work with others on campus to understand new initiatives, budget issues, strategic plans, and so on. They also work with donors and foundations as part of the larger community.
- Library user services, including borrowing, lending, document delivery, and so on, must use data to help decide on access policies.

These data include qualitative and quantitative information about the use of the collection and the building. Important data include circulation statistics, interlibrary loan requests, in-house circulation, and information on use of electronic resources. Other important data include examining access policies from other libraries.

- Public services such as reference and instruction must also be informed by user needs and behaviors, as well as by studies that advise on how to teach users to evaluate information, an essential higher-order thinking skill that is important for lifelong learning. Useful data for reference and instruction services include focus groups, questionnaires, and other user studies; statistical data on use of the collection; and analysis of requests for instruction, reference interactions, and modes of reference and instruction (in person, phone, online, chat, etc.).

- Collection development must be influenced by various kinds of data, including tracking funds, but also requests from users, collection use statistics, comparisons with other libraries, and information from vendors and publishers.

- Acquisitions also uses fund data and information from vendors and publishers. In addition, all the technical services need workload and productivity data to create the most efficient and best value-added processes.

- Cataloging (including processing, authority control, and database maintenance) uses workload and productivity statistics, but also database reports that help create better access, and various kinds of documentation and training material, and information from standards organizations (such as the creators of cataloging and encoding standards).

- Areas such as special collections, institutional repositories, digital initiatives, and so on rely on workload and usage data like other areas, but also on information gained from working with scholars and researchers on campus and elsewhere, as well as donors and collectors.

All the information gathered and used by an academic library requires the higher-order thinking skills of analysis and critical evaluation. The "analysis, synthesis, and evaluation" of information can lead to an evidence-based and accountable form of librarianship that uses qualitative and quantitative data thoughtfully. The cognitive, affective, and psychomotor domains are all essential to this EBL environment. Academic librarians must think, and think critically. They must feel— using multiple intelligences, including emotional intelligence to understand the needs of employees and library patrons. They must also *do*. Librarians may be best at doing, but it is the third step in the triad. First think, then feel. Analyze, synthesize, and evaluate, and then *do*, including teaching those higher-order skills to others.

# CHAPTER 5

# Managing and Marketing Resources

## 5.1 INTRODUCTION

Libraries began to hear about the need to do marketing in the 1980s and 1990s. It was a period that followed budget retrenchments of the 1970s, and a time when librarians began to realize that libraries were not universally regarded as something positive and valuable, organizations playing an essential function, and needing resources. Librarians awoke to the fact that funding agencies, governing bodies, elected officials, and institutional administrators did not necessarily understand what libraries and librarians do, and what they can provide in the way of access to resources and instruction in using them. In the mid-to-late 1990s, the emergence of the Internet had two competing effects: it allowed more-sophisticated and varied approaches to marketing, and it presented a new marketing challenge: the idea that "everything is on the Internet" and, moreover, that it is "free on the Internet."

While there was resistance to the idea of marketing in the past, it is now generally well accepted that all organizations—public, private, for-profit, and nonprofit—must market themselves in order to communicate with users about what they have to offer. That includes publicity, outreach, and creating a feedback loop that seeks information from users about how to enhance and improve services.

During the last 30 years, universities have become sophisticated at marketing. They use marketing techniques to reach and recruit potential students. Those techniques are based on knowledge of the potential student population, the institution's strengths, the strengths and marketing techniques of other colleges and universities, the economic environment, and the trends and predictions regarding education, communication, demographics, and other important factors. Universities have become more internally entrepreneurial, and departments and

*Managing Academic Libraries*
ISBN 978-1-84334-621-0
http://dx.doi.org/10.1016/B978-1-84334-621-0.00005-4

programs have learned to market themselves to compete for funding and students. Grant writing can even be seen as a form of marketing, in which teams and individuals make the case for their ability to carry out a project successfully.

All this means that library administrators and managers must understand the need for marketing, commit themselves and their organizations to do it, and know how to carry it out. A marketing culture is today as necessary as a culture of assessment, accountability, or learning in an academic library. Assuming that there is understanding of the need and commitment to carry out a marketing program, what are the steps in creating and managing one?

Marketing starts with knowledge of what the organization has to offer, and knowledge of the audience(s) for the organization's programs and services. After those things are accounted for, the library can choose tools for marketing and create its marketing and outreach service.

## 5.2 PROGRAM, SERVICE, AND AUDIENCE

What does an academic library offer students, faculty, and other users? Traditionally, the library offered a collection of books and other resources. Today's academic library still offers a collection, but more accurately offers discovery of resources and access to them. Academic libraries may market a number of different things:

- Access to thousands of electronic resources, including databases, scholarly journals, and reference tools;
- 24/7 access to electronic resources and reference help;
- Access to a substantial print and multimedia collection;
- Access to special collections and archives material in physical and digital formats;
- Quick access to material at other institutions through interlibrary loan;
- Liaison librarians to do reference, instruction, and collection development in a variety of subject areas;
- Embedded librarians, who work with teaching departments, with departmental office hours, and/or participation in teaching;

- Document delivery services;
- An institutional repository;
- Data curation services;
- Opportunities to work with the library on creation of digital archives of research material.

These are just a few of the most frequently encountered academic library activities. Who is our audience?

- Current and potential undergraduate and graduate students;
- Current and potential faculty;
- Our own librarians and library staff;
- University administrators;
- Other governing and funding bodies;
- The people of the city or state where we reside;
- Alumni of the institution;
- Scholars at other institutions;
- Consortia partners.

Each of these activities and each audience might benefit from a different approach. Governing bodies and funding agencies want to see accountability and good stewardship. Students want easily discoverable and usable resources and help when they need it. Faculty want a strong collection for research and teaching. Some of these groups may not "want" the things that would greatly benefit them.

## 5.3  MANAGING MARKETING

The first step for managers and administrators is to assign responsibility for marketing. The responsibility should be assigned to every library employee. Every employee has the responsibility of being an ambassador for the library. That includes frontline public services employees who have daily interactions with students and faculty. It includes librarians and administrators in their campus activities, when they encounter other faculty and administrators at committee meetings. It includes technical services employees who encounter a student looking lost in the hallway and stop to give directions or other assistance. Beyond these direct encounters, there is a marketing element to every decision and activity. Cataloging decisions and policies, circulation policies, collection development, design of references and instruction, all have a marketing component: what is the user model being employed and how is it being matched?

In assigning marketing responsibility to everyone, it is assumed that there is a marketing plan whose principles and guidelines are built into every library activity. Activities that are simply and specifically marketing, outreach, and communication should be the responsibility of one person (plus that person's staff), whether it is a marketing coordinator or part of the assignment of another appropriate person, such as an associate dean or associate director.

A marketing plan stems from the library mission and strategic plan, and requires an understanding of priorities on campus, funding sources, and the nature and needs of user communities. Marketing consists of assessing user needs and creating demand through publicity. It includes a feedback loop that is used for improving services and providing new ones. Marketing methods and channels include:

- Social media

  Most libraries use Facebook and Twitter. They may currently be the most effective means of quick and far-reaching communication. They can be used to announce events, encourage use of services, and generally be a constant and noticeable presence.

- Library Website

  It is hard to remember the time when libraries and other organizations did not have a Web presence. Along with Facebook and Twitter, the library Website is a prominent means of interacting and providing information to students, potential students, faculty, and others.

- Alumni association

  Alumni groups are used to working with colleges and departments on marketing and fundraising for the institution. Increasingly, libraries are becoming aware of the power of alumni to strengthen outreach to the community for fundraising and for understanding of the resources and programs that the library offers. Some institutions offer access to library resources (such as full-text databases) as an incentive for joining the alumni association.

- Student government
  Student government organizations offer an excellent opportunity for outreach to students regarding changes in service, funding issues, and creating support for the library.
- Presence at student recruitment events
  Colleges and universities routinely hold events to help recruit new students. The library should have a presence at these events, and the strength and excellence of the library should be considered a factor in attracting students to an institution.
- "Elevator speech"
  Since every college or university employee is an ambassador for the institution, the "elevator speech" refers to the idea that employees should be prepared to speak succinctly and positively about new and exciting developments and activities should they find themselves in an elevator with a member of the state legislator, a potential donor, etc.

## 5.4  ELEMENTS OF MARKETING

The literature of library marketing and outreach is vast and varied. There is a great deal of literature that makes the case for marketing, and offers definitions, general advice, and examples of approaches. Begum (2003) states that academic libraries "deliver products personally to the customer" (p. 1). Lowry (2005) urges academic libraries to be "ubiquitous" in meeting user needs.

Duke and Tucker (2007) urge libraries to develop a library marketing plan as a part of strategic planning. They give step-by-step instructions on developing such a plan. Estall and Stephens (2011) look at attitudes toward marketing of employees in academic libraries in the United Kingdom. Staff completed surveys and interviews that revealed that staff felt positive toward marketing while being uncertain about how to go about it. Galston, Kelsen Huber, Johnson, and Long (2012) argue that the need for demonstrating value goes beyond physical and virtual space, programming, outreach, and materials. Fourie and Ball (2012) discuss the need to market library resources and services and describe a marketing project that used social media, competitions, and prizes. Frumkin and Reese (2011) explore ways to market academic libraries as organizations that deliver information rather than as collections of resources. Germano (2010) recommends effective marketing as a way to strengthen the position of libraries in times of economic crisis. Recommendations include focusing on specific populations and creating a compelling narrative. Alansari (2013) surveyed academic library public relations efforts. The study found a commitment to public relations among the survey population but a lack of commitment to hiring staff to carry out this function. Alire (2007) introduces the idea of word-of-mouth marketing for academic libraries, including a success story of this kind of marketing campaign. Jamali, Moshabaki, Aramoon, and Alimohammadi (2013) investigate ways that libraries can establish and maintain relationships with users in a virtual environment. A questionnaire collected information on factors used in customer relationship management. James-Gilboe (2010) summarizes a study by ProQuest on academic library marketing, including best practices for libraries. Jayasundara, Ngulube, and Minishi-Majanja (2009) investigated the elements of service quality for libraries in Sri Lanka. Responsiveness, supportiveness, physical infrastructure, collection and access, technology, Web presence, and delivery of service were discovered to be among the dimensions of quality that can lead to user satisfaction. Sarjeant-Jenkins (2012) argue for academic library marketing as a means of securing adequate funding and making the best use of library spaces. Shafique (2009) explores "third-party theory," which views marketing as involving users, librarians, and administrators. Smith (2011) recommends that marketing activities be part of library strategic planning and that libraries have a permanent marketing committee. Spalding and Wang (2006) explore the value of marketing in academic libraries and its implementation in US libraries, finding that marketing helps libraries understand the needs and motives of faculty, students, and administrators.

A large body of literature explores specific library marketing efforts and techniques, particularly marketing for reference and similar services. Aguilar, Keating, Schadl, and Van Reenen (2011) describe efforts to expand reference services in expanded locations and a virtual environment, in an effort to "meet users where they are." Brown and Sen (2010) explore the use of a prospectus for undergraduate students as a marketing tool for academic libraries. A content analysis showed that the content of the prospectus regarding the library was a positive factor in students' decision making. Henry, Vardeman, and Syma (2012) discuss innovative ways to market reference services, including QR codes, videos, and roving reference. The videos and roving reference have been successful, but students have not adopted QR codes. Jones, McCandless, Kiblinger, Giles, and McCabe (2011) used the observations of frontline staff to make simple changes that improved marketing of library services. Changes included book displays that increased circulation and browsing. MacDonald, van Duinkerken, and Stephens (2008) discuss a marketing campaign to promote virtual reference service, including its design and implementation. Rudin (2008) reviews the history and current state of the outreach model of reference services, looking at roving and embedded librarianship as a means to deliver reference services. Sharman and Walsh (2012) describe a "roving librarian" project carried out at a UK university, which facilitated encounters on campus where students and faculty could receive help with library resources. Duke, MacDonald, and Trimble (2009) describe a project in which the library collaborated with business students to explore ways to market reference services. Torabi (2011) explores marketing techniques for ebooks, in a qualitative study that interviewed librarians and users. The study found an array of marketing techniques, including use of the library Website and creation of recommendation lists. Vasileiou and Rowley (2011) found a lack of focus in library marketing of ebooks and recommend a strategic approach to publicizing the availability of these materials. Williams and Peters (2012) describe the creation of a video to market a mobile search application.

The use of Facebook and other social media is being widely investigated as a channel for library marketing. Carter and Seaman (2011) discuss a study of more than 100 academic libraries that surveyed their outreach and marketing activities, finding the use of campus and library events along with blogs and other social media. Ayu and Abrizah (2011) look at the use of Facebook among academic libraries in Malaysia including the extent of use and the content of pages. Chan (2012) investigates the effectiveness of ways of using Facebook as a marketing tool for academic libraries, finding the use of the social aspect of Facebook most effective. Foster, Wilson, Allensworth, and Sands (2010) describe efforts to market LibGuides in an academic library. The guides were marketed using Facebook, Twitter, blogging, and email. The marketing had a significant impact, and email was found to be the method that has a measurable impact. Xia (2009) explores the use of Facebook groups for library marketing. The results of a study showed that these groups should be designed to reach faculty as well as students. Vucovich, Gordon, Mitchell, and Ennis (2013) analyzed library use of social media to understand how these marketing efforts were being received and used. O'Connor and Lundstrom (2011) look at the use of social media to market library services to students, using marketing concepts such as "customer and competitor assessment, market segmentation, identification of target behaviors, and the design and delivery of intervention techniques to alter those behaviors."

Many authors discuss general academic library marketing approaches, including their relationship to strategic planning. Empey and Black (2005) discuss a marketing campaign at an academic library based on the "@ your library" concept. The campaign used multiple channels to portray the library as "the beating heart of the university." Lorenzen (2010) explores academic library fundraising. Development officers were surveyed. Identifying potential donors was cited as the most important elements in successful fundraising. Donors can be identified and attracted through library special events. Nunn and Ruane (2011) describe the challenging marketing environment presented by increasing numbers of part-time and distance students, and techniques such as "partnering with marketing courses, roving reference, and highlighting staff expertise to raise awareness among users." Nwezeh (2010) explored awareness of library services among students at a Nigerian university. A questionnaire revealed that many students lack awareness of library resources and how to use them. Robinson (2012) discusses Peter Drucker's theory of marketing and its application to strategic planning and innovation in libraries, emphasizing understanding who customers are and what they need.

Madhusudhan (2008) discusses marketing issues in an environment in which library users pay membership fees. Maloney (2012) describes the use of displays to promote diversity and build relationships on campus. *Marketing Electronic Resources to Distance Students: A Multi-pronged Approach* (2007) investigates the needs of distance students, recommending an approach that includes "direct e-mail, a well-designed Website, work with faculty to embed a staged approach to developing students' knowledge of resources." Seeholzer (2011) describes the use of social events in the library as a means of marketing the library to students, including questions such as the role of these events in the library mission and the ability of social events to attract students to core library services. Martin (2012) discusses streaming video as a marketing method. Academic librarians reached out to faculty in this way and were successful in their efforts. Harris and Weller (2012) explore outreach for special collections librarians, discussing ways to raise awareness of these materials, including digitization, electronic finding aids, and collaboration with faculty. Strothmann and Antell (2010) explore ways of outreach and marketing to students in campus locations such as residence halls, including one librarian who lived in a residence hall as faculty-in-residence. These initiatives are in response to the fact that users can access library resources without going to the library. *Thinking Outside of the Library Box: The Library Communication Manager* (2007) discusses marketing of library electronic resources and the evolution of marketing in one library from a decentralized approach to the creation of a library communications manager position. Lin and Chiu (2012) describe the use of "photo-elicitation" as a means of gathering information about library "servicescape" design. Adeyemon (2009) discusses outreach services, specifically for students who lack technology competencies. The outreach services provide students with a "portable skills toolkit" that can be used in school, at work, and so on. Cannady, King, and Blendinger (2012) look at library outreach to adult learners, who are a growing student population. Cummings (2007) discusses efforts to expand the outreach aspect of liaison librarianship to create new partnerships on campus. Dennis (2012) explores outreach activities that can be done without a great deal of budget impact. A survey of listservs resulted in reports of successful outreach activities.

An important aspect of marketing is understanding the needs of different groups and populations of users. Mee (2013) discusses the efforts of a library in the United States to market resources to its students in international campuses, located in Kosovo, Croatia, and Dubai. Librarians used a variety of appropriate technology to reach these students and encourage the use of library resources. Mundava and Gray (2008) investigate ways to market library services to international students and faculty. Mu (2007) recommends ways of marketing library services to Asian students. The findings of a survey indicated that libraries must proactively market to Asian students, who may be unfamiliar with library resources and services in the United States. Walter (2005) explores collaboration between academic libraries and student services on outreach to students of color. The study revealed a number of opportunities for targeted library programming. Ye (2009) discusses library outreach to international students, finding that a review of the literature shows a need for a nuanced view that does not view all international students and student populations identically.

Library Websites are an important marketing tool. A number of authors have analyzed library Websites from a marketing point of view. Ziaei and Nooshinfard (2012) evaluate Websites of libraries in Iran to assess the marketing elements found there. Results show a lack of marketing efforts on these sites. Welch (2005) investigates the use of the library Website for marketing, including Website content and placement of links. Kaba (2011) examined academic library Websites of institutions in the United Arab Emirates. The study found that the Websites lacked a marketing element, including a lack of live support and information on things like copyright. Kaur (2009) investigated marketing via library Websites in Malaysia, examining the sites themselves and interviewing library managers. It was found that the Websites did not have marketing content.

## 5.5 PUTTING IT ALL TOGETHER

For academic library managers and administrators, their own experience and the evidence of the literature should make a number of things clear. The first is that the elements of marketing begin with knowing your programs and services and their value to users. The second element is understanding user populations and their needs. The third is being willing to "meet users where they are" literally and figuratively—to adapt programs to the expressed needs of users. Knowing those things also means making a strong commitment to communicating about them, creating a two-way channel of communication, using multiple methods to communicate, and using a feedback loop that allows programs to evolve as user needs change.

How can academic libraries put these elements in place? The steps in integrating and managing academic library marketing are:

- Begin with the learning organization that should be a part of academic library organizational development. Use that concept to create a mental model of how the library works: its place in carrying out the organizational mission, its obligation to be a factor in recruitment, its knowledge of users and their needs, its use of feedback to make programs better, and its continuous communication with users to make sure that they are aware of the services available to them.

- Assign every person in the organization the responsibility of knowing the library's programs well enough to be part of its marketing efforts, with the expectation that they will take any opportunity to communicate about those programs to others.

- Assign one or more people the more exclusive responsibility of managing the library's communication with users, including current and prospective students, faculty, alumni, governing bodies, and so on.

- Create a marketing plan that is multifaceted and continuously updated.

- Integrate that plan with the library's strategic planning process.

- Recognize that people in- and outside the institution will not have an accurate view of the library's programs unless there is constant, clear communication about those programs. Library users and other stakeholders require continuing communication through a variety of channels for them to understand the goals, challenges, and accomplishments of the library.

- Marketing includes publicity, but it also includes user studies, out-reach efforts, and creating a ubiquitous presence, online, at campus events, and in delivering services "where they are," whether in the library, in a residence hall, in a teaching department, or on the Web.

Managing marketing is managing relationships. Successful relationships are reciprocal and require commitment, the ability to listen, and an openness to change. This is true of the relationship between a library and its users as it is of a personal or professional relationship between two people. The idea of marketing in libraries was once regarded with dismay and distaste, when it seemed to imply an inappropriate commercial relationship. Over the past 30 years, library marketing has come to be seen as something essential and appropriate, the building of a relationship that can provide benefits to both libraries and their user communities.

# CHAPTER 6

# Managing Digital Collections

## 6.1 INTRODUCTION

In the current academic library environment, managing information *is* managing digital information. To a great extent, the terms "collection development" and "collection management" refer to building digital collections. They refer to managing the transition from print, to print plus online, to an environment where digital collections are the default, even though print and other physical media will have a place for some time to come. Managing this transition and managing digital collections have many aspects: funding, space, equipment, staffing, training, and technology. It means making choices, staying current, communicating with users, and collaborating with other libraries, other institutions, and others on campus.

Academic libraries are currently engaged in "spaces and services" discussions with others on campus, with the goal of creating student-centered spaces, academic success facilities (including campus units such as writing centers, as well as library reference and instruction activities), and spaces for faculty and student research. This means rethinking the role of print and other physical collections, and the collection assessment activity goes hand in hand with the spaces and services discussion.

Library collections affect every function and department: acquisition, bibliographic control, access, and use. Libraries are more than their collections, and collections are more than the things owned by or housed in the library. Nevertheless, the resources chosen by a library for its users are one of the central defining services in any library. Electronic or digital resources take a number of forms. These include commercially produced databases, ejournals, and ebooks, and other similar resources, including streaming audio and video and digital image collections. Other commercial eresources include collections of digitized primary source material. There are also increasing numbers of open-access journals, books, and archives. Another

*Managing Academic Libraries*
ISBN 978-1-84334-621-0
http://dx.doi.org/10.1016/B978-1-84334-621-0.00006-6

important kind of digital resource is locally produced research material and digital archives. Research material includes theses, dissertations, and faculty publications that may be housed in an institutional repository. It also includes research data that are preserved in a data repository. Other locally created resources include digitized special collections material, for example, letters, diaries, images, and other materials that pertain to a person, place, or thing.

## 6.2 ERESOURCES

Eresources have become common in library collections in the last 15 years. In the past 10 years, ejournals have become the default format for journals, and more and more titles are available electronically. Ebooks are increasingly common but not yet the default. Libraries have adapted their routines to accommodate these eresources. Library software has been adapted and created to handle these materials. Library catalogs and discovery tools have been optimized for access to eresources of all kinds. These resources allow access from anywhere at any time and have motivated libraries to create virtual reference service since users do not need to go to the library to use them. Eresources are expensive, but libraries have been able to take advantage of consortia discounts and to negotiate with vendors in other ways to achieve advantageous pricing. Faculty and students in all disciplines, but especially in the sciences, have demanded access to ejournals and databases.

In the current environment, academic libraries are facing a space crunch and are finding other uses for the space occupied by the print collection. Access to ejournals is not always stable enough to allow the print volumes to be withdrawn, but where there are stable archives, such as JSTOR, academic libraries are beginning to withdraw the print versions of titles. In addition, shared print repositories are being developed, so that libraries will be more willing to withdraw print.

## 6.3 DIGITAL COLLECTIONS

Academic libraries may potentially have a number of different kinds of digital resources. The first is the product of faculty and student research that may reside in a digital repository. These repositories are a product of the last 10 years and had their origin in the idea of electronic theses and dissertations. There are a number of available repositories, including Digital Commons, D-Space, and others. They provide server space and metadata for theses, dissertations, and for faculty's published works, generally a preprint version of journal articles and other materials. This allows open access to a large amount of research material that can be found with a Web search.

Another kind of digital resource is the "digital library," which may include a variety of things, including the institutional repository. Digital libraries bring together many different types of resources including digitized special collections material. While the rise of ejournals is somewhat associated with the sciences, a large area of digital library resources is digital humanities, which includes archives of primary source material in literature, history, and other areas. Digital humanities projects allow scholars to use primary sources without having to travel, making these resources available to users who previously would never have dreamed of using them. Digital humanities resources can be used for textual analysis, linguistic research, and for many other kinds of research in a variety of humanities disciplines. Libraries that create digital humanities projects may be collaborating with scholars on campus and at other institutions. Creating and maintaining these resources requires server space, IT support, and people with knowledge of a number of metadata schemes and encoding formats, including TEI and XML. There are large grants available for these projects, which require skill in applying for grants and carrying out the work that is funded.

## 6.4 COLLECTION ASSESSMENT

Libraries are completing the transition to an environment in which all or virtually all resources are online. This requires a process of collection assessment, which can refer to a number of activities, including weeding, determining what ejournal holdings are in stable archives, working with other institutions on shared storage, working with vendors on purchasing backfiles to allow withdrawal of print, and so on. Collection assessment requires careful coordination and communication. It requires a process for requesting and setting up projects. The process must include a way of prioritizing and a way to make sure that overlapping projects are not causing redundant effort. The transition from print to online requires space. The intersection of the "spaces and services" discussion and the collection assessment that goes along with it requires staging areas and swing space, since collections that are moving or being withdrawn must be housed somewhere during the process. Collection assessment also requires time and space for thoughtful decision-making.

## 6.5  THE ROLE OF MANAGERS AND ADMINISTRATORS

Managing digital collections implies many things, including funding, training, and workflow. It also implies that the library administration has made an organizational commitment to the creation and acquisition of digital resources. Administrators and managers must help the organization create a vision of the 21st-century library, and the role of collections and services in that library. Part of that vision is aligning the library's goals with those of the larger institution. Everyone in the library has a role in the management of digital resources, and administrators must get buy-in from the whole organization to move forward.

Funding issues include IT infrastructure, including hardware, software, and their maintenance. There are ongoing training needs for staff in every department. As there is turnover, or even new positions, it is essential to rethink every open position and hire strategically for the changing environment. In addition to rethinking positions, libraries must continuously rethink the organization itself. How are functions and departments aligned to deliver digital resources and services? Administrators must find appropriate collaborators for enriching digital collections. These include consortia, which might provide advantageous pricing for purchasing eresources, as well as cooperative digitization projects.

The management of digital collections obviously has a major collection development component. Managers must consider the allocation of funds for various formats of information. The transition from print to online resources brings into question the traditional split between funding for monographs and serials. It may no longer make sense to maintain that strict division, to maintain traditional funding formulas (eg, 70% for serials, 30% for monographs), and to maintain a single approach for all disciplines. The needs of the sciences for journals and the humanities for books may call for a more customized approach to funding, for example.

There is a great deal of literature on all aspects of managing digital collections. An important aspect of this topic is the needs and attitudes of users. Connaway and Dickey (2010) report that students in academic libraries seek full-text digital content from the academic library that serves the institution. They still value traditional library services and human sources of information but find digital collections more adaptable to work and study. Respondents to the survey also overwhelmingly reported using online resources such as the library's research databases and online journals, followed by the library online catalog. Mortimore (2006) advocates just-in-time acquisition accomplished through analysis of interlibrary loan requests. Evidence-based and demand-driven acquisitions are an important part of the digital environment, and this approach to collection development employs evidence to guide collection decision-making. Gerke and Maness (2010) discuss a survey of library users regarding digital collections. Use did not vary by their discipline but was correlated by frequency of use of the library Website. Hutton (2008) explores library service to distance students, recommending that libraries "pursue metadata standards to support cross-searching, collaborative projects, and development of eresource search software, which integrates with the library catalog." Huwe (2010) discusses the design of library spaces in the digital age. The library as place has taken on a new meaning in the digital era, and academic libraries are creating new spaces for students.

A crucial part of the digital landscape is open access material. Fernandez and Nariani (2011) state that "The open access publishing landscape is now international in scope and encompasses many approaches. Funding of OA initiatives is becoming increasingly important to libraries and has relevance for changing librarian roles" (p. 3). Open access is important as a collection stream but also as an organizational consideration.

The management of digital collections has a strong connection to the way libraries are organized and how work and responsibility are assigned. Jordan (2010) wrote that "OCLC Research provides the OCLC cooperative with an infrastructure and interactive process for helping libraries, museums and archives deal with the rapidly changing digital, global community" (p. 13).

The library has an important role to play in the digital educational environment. Mathews (2009, p. 19) writes that "Academic libraries must be able to express how the library is unique and how it adds value and contributes to the intellectual life of the university." That includes effective records management, including the management of digital records, which increases the operating efficiency and effectiveness of the academic library, reduces unnecessary, often hidden costs, ensures compliance with legislative requirements, provides litigation support, and is the basis of institutional memory. 2012 top 10 trends in academic libraries (2012) include communicating value, managing research data, and preserving digital collections. The article also explores data repositories and acquisition of electronic material. Maloney et al. (2010) found that leaders "perceive a significant gap between their current and preferred organizational cultures and that current organizational cultures limit their effectiveness." That gap may make it difficult to achieve the aims of creating data repositories and creating digital collections. "Adhocracy" is defined by Waterman (1992) as "any form of organization that cuts across normal bureaucratic lines to capture opportunities, solve problems, and get results." The current environment calls for some adhocracy, which may determine best practices and create new organizational patterns that work better. These new models and practices may apply to particular types of libraries or particular areas of academic libraries. Breakstone (2010) explores the availability of online resources for law libraries. Brenner, Larsen, and Weston (2006) "offer a strategy for adapting a library system to traditional archival practice." Conway (2008) defines a framework for the management of digital collections, which "offers an original model for evaluating the asset values of digital content produced or acquired in a university context."

One important aspect of digital collections is digitized material, which is created in-house or through a cooperative project. These may involve one or more academic libraries, other departments on campus, or a large organization such as Google. Breitbach, Tracey, and Neely (2002) describe a project to digitize slide images. Carlson and Young (2005) describe the Google Books digitization project, which began with Google collaborating with five large research libraries. "Framework for good digital collections: Version 3" released by NISO, IMLS (2008) reports on the release of NISO's framework for digital collections, which "establishes principles for creating, managing and preserving digital collections." Goldman (2011) explores the management of "born-digital" collections, including storage and access solutions. Gueguen and Hanlon (2009) discuss the management of digitization that is done at the point of use or demand. Huwe (2011) discusses the lawsuit filed against HathiTrust and its implications for the creation and use of digital collections. Jeng (2005) looks at the issue of usability of digital libraries, proposing a model for evaluating them, and finding "an interlocking relationship among effectiveness, efficiency, and satisfaction." Johnson and Mandity (2010) describe a collaborative digitization project involving two university libraries. Chen and Reilly (2011) discuss the use of preservation metadata in a digital library. Nelson (2012) investigates the inclusion of "born-digital" materials in library special collections. Nikolaidou, Anagnostopoulos, and Hatzopoulos (2005) discuss a digital library that supports research in a medical school, describing requirements for creating objects and searching. Oehlerts and Liu (2013) present options for digital preservation including practices, tools, and technologies. Zorich (2007) discusses the need for preservation of digital objects and for cultural heritage organizations to maintain their stewardship role. Foulonneau et al. (2006) describe the CIC metadata portal project, which explored sharing information about digital collections among universities. Hurford and Runyon (2011) describe the Bracker Collection of horticultural material at Ball State University Libraries, which "posed significant challenges to traditional archival collection processing procedures and existing digital collection building workflows." Seo and Zanish-Belcher (2005) observe that a variety of issues go into preservation decision-making as it relates to special collections, including the paramount role of priority setting as well as effective communication. Hubbard (2001) describes the programs of the Getty Research Institute, including the creation of a single discovery system, and a review of digital asset management. Kretzschmar and Potter (2010) discuss issues in digital humanities projects, including data storage, changing media and technology, and the unique challenges presented in maintaining digital archives. Lampert and Vaughan (2009) use a case study and survey to investigate academic library digitization programs, finding that "potential success factors" include "staff skill sets, funding, and strategic planning." Lopatin (2010) looks at metadata for digital projects, including issues like interoperability, user-created metadata, and staffing. Prilop, Westbrook, and German (2012) describe a multidepartment workflow for digitization, including "the collaborative planning process ... the rewards and challenges of tackling such a project," and "lessons learned." Rafiq and Ameen (2013) explored digitization practices in university libraries of Pakistan and found that one-third of libraries surveyed had digitization programs. Rentfrow (2006) explores the challenges of producing digital thematic research collections, drawing on experience from particular projects. Wolski (2011) investigates archiving of research data and states that although "libraries have a history of designing discovery systems, new research paradigms" present challenges and opportunities. Worthey (2009) explores issues in archiving digital content, including its role in scholarly communication. Watanabe (2007) explores the promotion of eresources to library users. Wu (2011) "presents a vision of a collaborative, digital academic law library" and explores issues such as copyright. Zambare et al. (2009) describe the challenges of migration from a print to an online environment. Zimmerman and Paschal (2009) write of an exploratory study in which the usability of Websites was assessed.

Another essential aspect of managing digital collections is the organization and administration of library functions and departments, including the general collection development process.

The literature on this topic explores the print-to-online transition, the management of eresources, and the roles of traditional library functions such as cataloging, acquisitions, reference, and instruction. Breeding (2012) addresses the management of library collections in the current environment, including various models of acquisition of ebooks and journals. Carr and Collins (2008) explore the management of digital resources and the transition from a print to an online environment, including acquisition and licensing. Chadwell (2011) discusses gaming in public and academic libraries, including the field of new media studies. Collins (2009) investigates electronic resource management workflows, including planning, staffing, and communication. Demas and Miller (2012) explore the use of collection management, including "disposition of withdrawn materials, life-cycle management retention, and education and community support." DeVoe (2006) defines the challenges of the electronic environment, including the rapid growth in availability of eresources. Farmer (2009) discusses digital reference resources, "focusing on subscription databases: assessment, selection, acquisition, Web presentation and maintenance, archiving and preservation, and de-selection." Flatley and Prock (2009) explore the need for a defined process for selecting and evaluating eresources. Angel (2011) provides a gap analysis of the digital collections department at an academic library. Blummer and Kenton (2012) is a review of the literature on ebooks from 2005 to 2011 to find best practices, which include cataloging, usage statistics, and promotion of these materials. Gregory, Weber, and Dippie (2008) explore the role of technical services librarians in the management of digital resources, including "creative uses of the catalog, participating in the creation and improvement of metadata standards, enhancing the development of, and access to digital collections; knowledge management collaborations with library colleagues, academic departments, and other organizations; database development and instruction; teaching and reference activities; and technology support." Gómez, López, Prats, and Rovira (2004) describe an academic library's management of digital resources, including separate systems for commercial ebooks and journals and a repository of material such as dissertations. Horava (2010a) explores collection management in the current environment, including "core values, scholarly communication issues, acquisition activities, access and delivery issues, and innovation." Horava (2010b) considers collection management from the point of view of environmental sustainability and use of space. Kulp and Rupp-Serrano (2005) explore the acquisition of eresources, including funding, staffing, decision-making, and workflow, finding various answers in a survey of 24 academic libraries. Johns (2003) explores the problem of supporting and managing both print and digital collections. Kichuk (2010) is a case study of the growth of eresources in academic libraries, finding stages of development corresponding to different types of resources: bibliographic, full text, and reference. Lewis (2007) discusses the disruption of traditional academic library service that is the result of the "application of digital technologies to scholarly communications." The author advises that libraries "complete the migration from print to electronic collections ... retire legacy print collections ... redevelop library space ... reposition library and information tools, resources, and expertise ... and ... migrate the focus of collections from purchasing materials to curating content." Lindsay, Kemper, and Oelschlegel (2012) present the advantages of purchasing electronic backfiles and removing print collections in a medical library. Maxey-Harris (2010) investigates eresources that enhance research into diversity and multiculturalism, finding a rapid increase in subscriptions to these materials by ARL libraries in recent years. Price (2009) discusses electronic collection development for libraries with limited funds, including open access resources, negotiation with vendors, and forming consortia. Safley (2006) describes the role of eresources and consortia purchasing in improving collections and services in the library of a scientific research institute. Schonfeld (2010) discusses the future of print collections in an increasingly digital environment. Shearer, Klatt, and Nagy (2009) investigate methods of choosing and evaluating collections of core ejournals for a medical school library. Smith (2006) discusses development of electronic collections and methods of assessing collections, including digital and electronic collections, to determine whether they match institutional goals. Sinn (2012) surveyed the scholarly literature in history to discover the extent of use of digital resources, resulting in guidelines for the creation of digital material. Skekel (2008) analyzes the role of libraries in producing and providing access to digital collections, finding that libraries are "expanding their traditional roles of collecting, organizing, and providing access to resources. Their new roles include creating content and in some ways, also creating the access." Southwell and Slater (2012) examine the use of technology for accessing digital materials, surveying Websites to determine whether digital materials were accessible using screen reader technology, and finding that about 42% were accessible in this way. Sowell, Boock, Landis, and Nutefall (2012) is a case study of managing government in the transition from a print to a digital environment, recommending a balance between the needs of the library and its users and the requirements of the Federal Depository Library Program. Staiger (2012) reviews the research on the use of ebooks, discovering that academic library users do not read ebooks in their entirety but refer to particular pieces of information. Stevens (2006) describes the planning process for a completely electronic library, including changes to "collections, budgets, staffing, services, and buildings." Stewart (2012) explores digital preservation and presents ideas such as collaboration with others on campus in these efforts. Taber and Conger (2010) describe the involvement of a cataloging department in creation of an institutional repository, which "brought opportunities to redefine its perceived role," including the "creative repurposing of staff, students, and skills in order to integrate these new formats and processes (both physical and digital) into departmental workflows." Tennant (2001) discusses XML and its role in creating and managing digital objects. Tharani (2012) explores digitization for off-campus communities, in which "academic libraries can reposition themselves as responsive and relevant in the face of a changing digital services landscape." Updike and Rosen (2006) describe the creation of a digital image database for teaching, learning, and research. Vasileiou, Hartley, and Rowley (2012) report on research into methods and criteria for selecting ebooks. These criteria include price, platform, and a number of other items.

## 6.6 CONCLUSIONS

Libraries are always in transition. Academic libraries find themselves in the position of maintaining collections and services that support teaching and research as they exist now, but also helping their institutions carve a path into the emerging world of online teaching, learning, and research. These things have existed for nearly 20 years, and libraries have become increasingly adept at supporting online education and providing online resources, but the environment continues to shift rapidly, and it is not always easy to find the best path through competing choices in a somewhat chaotic environment.

Academic library managers and administrators have a clear role in managing digital resources in this era of transition. That role includes:

- Creating dialog and partnerships with others on campus and in the educational and information technology community to create digital resources, purchase commercial eresources at an advantageous cost, create and acquire useful discovery systems, and create a student-centered physical environment, including a reduced footprint for the physical collection.
- Creating a more flexible library organization that allows learning and collaboration, which is inclusive, and which recognizes expertise that can be used and developed to manage digital collections.
- Recognizing the continuous environment of transition and encouraging the organization to become comfortable with that environment.
- Recognizing and cultivating areas of collection strength that can be an essential part of the digital environment.
- Being a part of the open access movement, encouraging creation of open access publications, and providing easy access to them.

## CHAPTER 7

# Learning Organizations and Competitive Intelligence

## 7.1 INTRODUCTION

Strategic planning centers on the issues of the proper goals of the individual academic library and how policy can be written to achieve these goals. The process is not purely quantitative and policy driven because strategic planning recognizes stakeholder diversity and encourages full participation in a commonsense way. Douglas Birdsall (1997)wrote, "Strategic planning emphasizes environmental scanning and goal setting, whereas organizational development relies on intervention techniques, such as benchmarking and team building." Corporate strategy would include all facets of operations, including production, finance, and marketing. Strategic planning began to be applied to institutions of higher education when funding crises would determine which programs would survive and at which levels they would be funded. Since the late 1970s, it became evident that diversity is required in strategic planning. For example, in many academic libraries, strategic planning is initiated by senior administrators who require all campus units to submit plans for the overall purpose of developing planning cycles. This system of planning is linked to the allocation of resources and is meant to align the library's mission and goals closely with those of the university. The rational activity of planning, then, coexists with the politics of academe and is based on participative management.

In order that the organization develops so that strategic planning is successful, the concept of information sharing must become an integral component of organizational development. In the article entitled "Information Sharing, an Exploration of the Literature and Some Propositions," Tom Wilson (2010) described a matrix model as a guide

*Managing Academic Libraries*
ISBN 978-1-84334-621-0
http://dx.doi.org/10.1016/B978-1-84334-621-0.00007-8

to information sharing in organizations and gave advice as to the circumstances under which information sharing may take place easily, rather than artificially created circumstances under which sharing is difficult to achieve (paper 440). Leadership has a role in encouraging information sharing and in the development of an information sharing culture, which he writes, "itself may be related to leadership." Components of an information sharing culture are risk, reward, trust, leadership, and a positive organizational environment. Such components are also ways in which to study managing strategic planning in the academic library. In many academic libraries, senior administrators require campus units to submit plans that will be used in developing planning cycles. This system of planning, linked to the allocation of resources, is meant to ensure that the library's mission and goals are closely aligned with the mission and goals of the university. Therefore planning coexists with the politics of academe. Birdcall (2001) suggests that the three main political strategies for maximizing planning outcomes are to build upon the diversity of stakeholder interests, form alliances and coalitions for the advancement of the library's own interests, and market the planning document. One of the key responsibilities of the manager is to help subordinates develop their administrative potential. To do this, the manager needs to understand, motivate, and inspire. The manager can ask for contributions to the planning document and incorporate the feedback received. The value of mission statements, goals, and objectives can be integrated into the planning document and, later, policy by use of the strengths, weaknesses, opportunities, and threats (SWOT) tool, where the manager designs a matrix of SWOT and staff analyze the organization's strengths and weaknesses, as well as the opportunities and threats faced both internally and externally.

Organizational culture is a set of shared values and beliefs that can guide and constrain the behavior of the members of the group. Therefore, the mentality and personality of the group must be considered in the administrative process of strategic planning. The manager will know what the group values are and, if they are positive, foster them. On the other hand, the need to form a different organizational culture that will accept change in the work environment may be obvious. New employees might be chosen because of how they embody the organizational culture and also their potential to bring new ideas into the environment. A positive organizational culture is necessary to make the learning organization work. The norms, values, and behaviors of the organization are its culture, and culture includes the attitudes of employees. The organizational culture has a significant impact on how employees handle the type of change that is required for growth. If an organization is considered by employees to be progressive and dynamic, they are more likely to accept change. This does not mean that skepticism is thwarted, but that innovation is rewarded. The team environment fosters this kind of problem-solving, and is the more common overlay to bureaucratic structures in academic libraries. The organizational structure of a learning organization is organic in that there is flexibility of job definitions and duties. It is adaptable; there is lateral and horizontal flow of communication, influence is based on authority of knowledge, not position, and there is a system-wide orientation. Employees become committed not only to the profession but to the organization. The manager considers the need for staff education and training and manager education and training.

## 7.2  MORE ON THE LEARNING ORGANIZATION

Textbook authors Robert Stueart and Barbara Moran (2007) cited Peter Senge as the originator of the approach to management known as the learning organization (p. 35). Learning organizations facilitate open communication and decision-making at lower levels so that the culture is receptive to change rather than controlled at the top. They allow the people of the organization to make sense of their organization, providing them with an identity and impetus to work together. This is best accomplished by acclimating new hires to the organization's shared vision and mission statements and by providing the opportunity to learn new job skills from peers. The learning organization focuses on constant learning because environments rapidly change and academic libraries must meet these challenges by continually engaging themselves in the community. The learning organization requires the building of a mentoring culture. In the Eight Hallmarks of a Mentoring Culture, Lois Zachary (2011) stated that if the following performance variables are present, the culture is more likely to be self-sustainable. These eight hallmarks begin with accountability, which helps the employee to set goals, clarify expectations, and define roles and responsibilities. Alignment is shared understanding that fits naturally with the organization's values, its practices, mission and goals. Communication, fundamental to achieving mentoring excellence, creates value and demand for learning opportunities. Value and visibility address role modeling, reward, recognition, and celebration. Demand addresses the fact that employees seek mentoring as a way to develop themselves as mentors. Effective mentoring cultures establish safety nets to avoid stumbling blocks within the organization. Such cultures enable the employee to move forward. Because safety nets involve anticipating challenges for the employee, they are the mark of a resilient and responsive organization.

## 7.3  THE COMMUNITY AND USER FOCUS

In an article entitled "Beyond Information: The Academic Library as an Educational Change Agent," Alan Bundy (2004) wrote, "Mass higher education, flexible delivery, student centered and problem based learning, information literacy and other graduate attributes, are accelerating curricular and pedagogical change in progressive universities. Academic librarians need to partner academic teachers and others in that change, an impetus for which in Australia and New Zealand is the *Information literacy framework* and the Institute for Information Literacy. With their commitment to the free flow of information and ideas, they must also demonstrate a commitment to education which liberates, and should be willing to be held to account for graduates who are not able to function effectively in the complex information environment of the 21st century. The mission of the university library must therefore move beyond excellence in information identification, acquisition, organization, access and skills development. It should be described and asserted in educational, not informational, terms" (p.1). Bundy added that librarians have always been educators.

## 7.4  THE CANARY IN THE MINE

In 2006 the Association of College and Research Libraries (ACRL) in the United States stated that a combination of constrained budgets and the competitive domain of information production impacts every library in some way. Major research libraries may still be able to invest in collections, but most university and college libraries face tradeoffs between print publications and digital resources, and many journal subscriptions have been cut. Academic librarians are negotiating licensing agreements with digital content providers in order to acquire access to what are considered the important digital collections supporting subjects taught; they are reprofiling approval plans, or implementing new software to provide federated searching for students—students who may now consider the library as primarily book centered and second to Internet research. Yet ironically, the academic library has become more transparent to its parent with the high cost of providing faculty and students with access to scholarly resources via licensing agreements with electronic journals, databases, and other digital resources. ACRL referred academic libraries as "canaries in the mine" (Canaries were once regularly used in coal mining as an early warning system. Toxic gases such as carbon monoxide, methane, or carbon dioxide in the mine would kill the bird.) In this metaphor, for-profit institutions that cater to market demand and do not make a commitment to expanding or preserving human knowledge are the poisonous gasses, and for-profit institutions are the fastest-growing segment of postsecondary education. For-profit education providers will often contract out both the library and faculty to deliver information with speed and efficiency and immediate practical application. The way in which students are using digital information has been driving the change. To keep the canary alive in the academic library faced with drastic cuts to state budgets, the crisis in higher education itself must be solved. The development of enrollment policies along with factors of pricing, retention, and financial aid will all come into the play of strategic planning and organizational development. Nevertheless, scholars affiliated with the institution require access to full text resources, so the traditional collection development activities of collecting, preserving, as well as providing access to datasets, remain. Because of consolidation trends in the publishing industry and the fall of small publishers and publications, shared collection development practices take center stage. The manager will develop skills on how to improve the functioning of the organization for shared collection development practices and by doing so increase the satisfaction of people who are engaged in the workplace, and satisfaction is positively correlated with productivity.

## 7.5 COMPETITIVE INTELLIGENCE AND THE PUBLISHING INDUSTRY

Competitive intelligence is the action of defining, gathering, analyzing, and distributing intelligence about products, customers, and competitors. Competitive intelligence is also a discipline that uses legal and ethical means for discovering new knowledge about the external environment to facilitate decision-making. The use of competitive intelligence in library management may help mitigate the difficult climate facing universities today. It can improve how the academic library is positioned within the organization and assist the manager to make better management decisions. Competitive intelligence can be linked to user studies and is part and parcel of good environmental analysis. Competitive intelligence can help the university library move forward when an ongoing information technology strategy process and funding cycle are effectively integrated at the broader university level. Common management tools such as SWOT analysis, scenario analysis, and Porter's five forces analysis all feed into the notion of information as intelligence. Some tools are more rigorous than others, and many were developed for industry profits rather than educational institutions. Academic library managers know that resource provision for subjects offered by the university is not all about those subjects that are most profitable in terms of tuition dollars, that a balanced collection serves the university community best. For example, most large universities in the United States are land grant institutions, and land grant institutions were established to train teachers. For 150 years, land grant institutions were meant to benefit communities around the world through civic engagement and democratic principles. Unfortunately, this engagement has eroded. The goal of competitive intelligence in library management is to gain a solid understanding of the publishing industry, specific companies, their key products, trends, and competitors, and this goal can be engaged to meet mission statements.

# CHAPTER 8

# Managing the Benefits of Academic Libraries

## 8.1 INTRODUCTION

What are the benefits of academic libraries? They include:

- Access to resources that support teaching and research;
- Use of funds as an information subsidy that is distributed to all members of the community;
- Spaces for learning and collaboration;
- A core of experts whose values include cultural competence, multiple literacies, technological aptitude, and expertise in a range of activities.

Libraries perceive themselves as an unquestioned good in society, and few would argue with this. In an academic context, lip service, at least, is given to the idea that the library is "the heart of the university." The actual benefits of academic libraries include large and well-organized collections of research material (whether or not the collection is ever considered "adequate"), long hours, comfortable spaces, and helpful experts. Libraries provide programs, services, and collaborations that partner with and support research and teachings. We can imagine a college or university without a library. Some higher education administrators have naively done so. Such an institution would rely on information purchased or provided freely by individuals. It would be hard to imagine the lives of students, faculty, and scholarly publishers without the role played by libraries in subsidizing information, interpreting, and giving access to it.

Managing these beneficial effects is managing everything we do. Gorman (2003) writes that, "Just as the common good in society demands equilibrium between individualism and order—between the demands of the self and the good of all—the practice of librarianship demands equilibrium between tradition and innovation, the old

*Managing Academic Libraries*
ISBN 978-1-84334-621-0
http://dx.doi.org/10.1016/B978-1-84334-621-0.00008-X

and the new, the needs of the many and the needs of minorities or individuals. The task is to use the three lanterns of our values (service, intellectual freedom, equity of access), our code of ethics, and the Eightfold Path and concomitant virtues to light our way as we wrestle with the issues, dilemmas, and problems of the age in which we live and work. In negotiating these issues, we must always seek harmony, balance, and the middle way" (p. 141). Gorman identified eight central values of librarianship that are appropriate to how libraries are managed. They are stewardship, service, intellectual freedom, privacy, rationalism, commitment to literacy and learning, equity of access, and democracy. The idea of the common good and the library faith can be applied to 21st-century practice of management of academic libraries. Developing peer relationships, resolving conflicts, motivating staff, establishing information networks, allocating resources, and making decisions are all managerial skills that can be built on the foundation of the values that Gorman lists. Mintzberg (1990) emphasizes the role of management in putting values into practice and observes that, "No job is more vital to our society than that of the manager. The manager determines whether our social institutions will serve us well or whether they will squander our talents and resources" (p. 20).

In some sense, the library's mission and its benefits are the same. The beneficial effects of the academic library are incorporated in its mission statement. The mission statement states the purpose of the library, eg, assisting the university community to reach its potential in academic achievement, economic development, and personal growth. The critical roles of advancing the teaching, learning, research, and service missions of the institution are the foundation of what it means to manage well. In academic libraries, staff must possess a personal teaching philosophy in the context of information literacy in higher education. In order to manage the beneficial effects of the academic library in the lives of students, the multiple and dynamic nature of college literacy must be understood. In the United States, the focus of literacy is on the individual. The learner becomes a more productive and independent person by reading, writing, and computing. The meaning of adult literacy in developing countries in Latin America,

Africa, and Asia, however, is literacy for community development. Beder (1997) writes that "Rather than focusing on individuals, literacy for community development focuses on the benefits of adult literacy education to a community. The presumption is that if through collective action a community is able to solve the problems that create poverty, poor health, and oppressive conditions, all the individuals will benefit." A community development approach to literacy holds promise for staff development and teamwork, and lessens the isolation imposed by bureaucracy. This community development approach has a number of aspects, which are explored below.

## 8.2  FOCUS ON THE USER

Engaging with texts in ways particular to academic disciplines is called reflective literacy. Acting on the insights gained from reflection is where development occurs. The 21st-century learner must find opportunities for learning through social interaction. The user population of academic libraries is diverse, and the library needs resources to support a socially inclusive program. Academic librarians can reach users by being multiculturally competent. Multicultural competence promotes social understanding, inclusion, affirmation, and harmony in a pluralistic world. A user focus is one of the most powerful ways of managing the benefits of academic libraries. Engaging with users and measuring the outcomes of those interactions (in terms of retention, graduation rates, academic success, and information literacy) are essential aspects of communicating value.

## 8.3  FOCUS ON MANAGEMENT

Retention of students and high graduation rates are a benefit of good management of a college or university. A benefit of academic libraries can be their effect on retention. Emmons and Wilkinson (2011) studied the impact of the academic library on student persistence. They explored the relationship between traditional library input and output measures of staff, collections, use, and services with retention and six-year graduation rates, using members of the

Association of Research Libraries as a population. The authors found that an increase in the ratio of librarians to students indicates a positive relationship with retention and graduation rates. These findings strengthen the role of evidence-based practice in librarianship.

Evidence-based practice establishes targets for the short and long term, analyzing and evaluating the environment, weighing courses of action, considering advantages and disadvantages of each. An important aspect of evidence-based practice and of the management of the benefits of the library is budgeting. Budgeting should be based on evidence of needs, trends, and spending patterns. Managers implement plans by allocating resources, including funds and people, and putting procedures in place for evaluation of the plan.

Budgeting is set in the context of the past, present, and future. Budgeting and planning are done in a yearly cycle, and the final step is evaluating the results of planning. That cycle strengthens decision-making, and, if the budget must be cut, those decisions can be made in several ways, including needs analysis, cost analysis, resource analysis, or impact analysis, using the evaluation phase of the budget cycle. Reducing human resources is the least desirable way to make budget cuts. The impact on student retention is one of the beneficial aspects of well-staffed academic libraries. Relationship building is the heart of academic library practice. Students will clearly be affected when staff are cut, and this will affect the library's role in the university.

## 8.4 FOCUS ON HUMAN RESOURCES

A library is not its collection. As access and delivery of resources become more efficient, and as it becomes clear that only a tiny portion of any collection is unique, it becomes more obvious that library employees are more important than the collection. W. Edwards Deming, who was trained as a statistician, wrote, "in any given organization, 95% of all employees perform well and only 5% of the workers cause significant problems in the workplace" (Rasch, 2004, p. 408). Solving the problems of a mere 5% of the workforce is something that can be accomplished. Another important element of human resources management is to question underlying assumptions. Powell

(1989) quoted Goldhor, who stated that the overarching question of management is "what effect would, or does, each administrative decision—regarding services or operations—have on the library's clientele?" Management must provide a model of engagement with users in the design of jobs for employees. Performance appraisals must provide the opportunity for employees to describe their contributions to the organization and elicit feedback on how employees can be better supported by management.

## 8.5  FOCUS ON COLLEGIALITY

Collegial management motivates employees. Although it is easier to express the spirit than the application of collegiality, the common elements of collegial management are group autonomy, personal responsibility, and voluntary group participation. Moreover, the director of the academic library must be able to delegate authority. Professionals do not generally need "supervision" because they have a system of peer review. They still need mentoring, however. The leader keeps the group on track, and participation is encouraged and rewarded. Leadership is shared. The common ground is service to the users of the academic library. Collegiality need be articulated as a statement of values in the mission statement of the academic library.

Information literacy, an essential skill of an educated workforce, has a component of trust. The concept of trust has much in common with users' perception of value in the library environment, and value shares much with collaboration. Aharony's (2011) research on organizational knowledge sharing compared two groups of Israeli librarians, academic and public. Personality and situational characteristics were found to influence participants' knowledge sharing in the organization. Similarly, Tan and Higgins (2002) found that the provision of digital resources was only part of the management puzzle, and that fostering a learning culture for staff and students was equally important. The researchers concluded that the library had a majority of the characteristics of the learning organization, but that new attitudes needed to be cultivated and greater trust fostered among employees in order to leverage the library's knowledge assets. Staff were rewarded based on their ability to collaborate, champion learning, and share knowledge. Castiglione (2008) found intrinsic motivation to be the primary driver of individual creativity as well as organizational learning. He wrote that "Library administrators are directly responsible for creating and sustaining an organizational culture that facilitates the intrinsic motivation of all library staff members" (p. 159). Budd (1998) says that "one all encompassing view of society probably does not serve the aims of higher education." Diversity in education for librarianship is growing as the need to serve underserved populations grows. A university library guarantees all students full and open access to the library's collections and services. This guarantee does not change for distance education students, and so digital resources are proliferating. The success of the academic library depends on the ability to adjust products and services to correspond to user needs.

## 8.6  FOCUS ON STRATEGIC PLANNING

Strategic planning is the process of creating goals and objectives that advance the organizational mission. One of the main goals of the academic library is to create lifelong learners. This is certainly one of the prominent benefits of academic libraries. As part of its strategic planning, the library can establish a goal of providing literacy training to students. Strong information literacy programs will benefit the library's strategic planning efforts because it aligns the library's goals with that of the university.

## 8.7  RETURN ON INVESTMENT

Return on Investment (ROI) is a way of measuring value and of communicating the value of educational institutions such as libraries to their governing and funding bodies. A number of studies have attempted to show ROI for academic libraries. Oder, Blumenstein, Hadro, Rapp, and Zisko (2010) explored ROI for libraries from grant income. Coyle (2006) looks at the difficult question of ROI for libraries in terms of technology, including digitization and the value of cataloging, finding that funds for technology have a high ROI. "IMLS Grants to Support ROI Study, Digitization, More" (2009) discusses funding for ROI studies by the Institute of Museum and

Library Services (IMLS). Mays, Tenopir, and Kaufman (2010) report on such a grant project, the "Value, Outcomes, and Return on Investment of Academic Libraries project," which was called "Lib-Value." Sidorko (2010) examines approaches to ROI for academic libraries, including the various methodologies that are available. ROI is an issue in accreditation for universities, and Stielow (2011) looks at this issue in the online education environment. Tenopir (2010) looked at the value of ejournals and ROI for grant funds. Grzeschik (2010) also looks at ROI in terms of grant funds, in two German academic libraries, at the Berlin School of Library and Information Science and Humboldt University, Berlin.

## 8.8 COMMUNITY INFORMATICS

Community informatics (CI) looks at the interaction of information technology and communities, including the use of information technology to benefit communities. Averweg and Leaning (2011) explore the meanings of "community" and the political aspect of CI. Goodwin (2007) looks at CI's "distinct agenda for change" and the role of the Internet in creating social change.

Shin and Shin (2012) examine the relationship of information technology and urban spaces. This has relevance for academic library "spaces and services" discussions and the creation of spaces for students and others. Stillman and Linger (2009) discuss the theoretical basis of CI, seeing an opportunity "to address both social and technological issues in its theoretical framework," which has implications for academic libraries and their expressions of value. Williams, Bishop, Bruce, and Irish (2012) examine CI in library and information science (LIS) curricula, discussing ways that LIS students can become involved in communities and their information needs. The concept of community encourages practitioners and researchers to understand the significance of ethnic and cultural associations, and to develop professional interests that will provide the frameworks for social meaning and action. Academic library communities share practices physically and electronically. Arshad and Ameen (2010) observes that libraries in developing countries are significantly affected by ongoing information and communications technology (ICT) developments, from basic infrastructure to collections, services, and human resources. She states that all segments of the community need vision and preparedness to turn challenges into opportunities. Globally, CI addresses poverty reduction through the use of technology. The communal dimension focuses on developing strategies for using ICT to enable and empower those living in physical communities around the world. It can be used as a conceptual approach for the management of academic libraries.

## 8.9 CONCLUSIONS

Managing the benefits of academic libraries includes identifying and communicating those benefits. It demands a culture of evidence and assessment and a willingness to question and discard assumptions. It demands engagement with users and a willingness to listen and to act on feedback to make changes. Managing the benefits also means working with library employees to make sure that training, policies, practices, and processes all adhere to the library's values, mission, and vision. The challenges for the manager are considerable, including:

- Understanding the benefits provided by the library and creating and communicating those benefits;
- Understanding the needs of the communities served;
- Acquiring understanding of methodologies such as ROI and practicing evidence-based librarianship;
- Articulating expectations for employees that include engagement with users;
- Making decisions in a way that supports and strengthens the benefits of the library;
- Creating a planning and budgeting cycle that includes an evaluation phase.

In managing benefits, managers must also recognize competitors and be strategic in identifying a role for the library as a place and a program.

# CONCLUSION

It is clear that academic library collections attract scholars, graduate students, government support, and donor funding. Collections add prestige to the institution through their research potential. Research based on collections can change the practice of library services to students and faculty. Formats that support multiple literacies are available to faculty—this expertise supports learners in the distributed online environment. Since the political and economic considerations of library collections revolve around the institutional affiliations of that library, access to resources that support teaching and research are paramount. Teaching, research, and service have always been the raison d'être of the academic library. Academic libraries must be managed well in order to reach the potential of full access—by managers who value students from diverse backgrounds and possess business acumen. Internal operating costs of research libraries are more than twice as high as their acquisition budgets. As everyone knows, the largest piece of the budget pays salaries. Nevertheless, the welfare of staff comes before the acquisition of resources. Academic library managers must intentionally plan services based on their clientele as well as for different kinds of learners, regardless of country of origin—this is how academic libraries can align the library's mission to the university's mission and provide benefit to the community served. Such a purpose demonstrates an acknowledgement of how the learner has a need for social, interactive, and collaborative learning spaces. Learners from diverse backgrounds bring their own interpretations of information to collections. In the future, collection management will focus on preserving and cataloguing social networking sites and other emerging digital forms. Regardless of format, the management of academic libraries will continue to focus on service to the users—the students and the faculty. Clearly, the academic library and its collection allow staff to mentor students as well as retain them. Service quality is determined by the library's staff efforts to care for the users' information needs, to practice evidenced-based librarianship, and to articulate an expectation for employees to engage. Decisions that support and strengthen the benefits of the library necessitate a multidimensional approach to problem solving.

# REFERENCES

2012 top ten trends in academic libraries. *College & Research Libraries News*, *73*(6), (2012), 311–320.

Adeyemon, E. (2009). Integrating digital literacies into outreach services for underserved youth populations. *Reference Librarian*, *50*(1), 85–98. http://dx.doi.org/10.1080/02763870802546423.

Agnello, M. F. (2008). Freirean cultural lenses for promoting future teacher literacy knowledge: dominant literacy discourses and majority interns in a minority high school. *Journal of Thought*, *43*(1–2), 107–130.

Aguilar, P., Keating, K., Schadl, S., & Van Reenen, J. (2011). Reference as outreach: meeting users where they are. *Journal of Library Administration*, *51*(4), 343–358. http://dx.doi.org/10.1080/0193. 0826.2011.556958.

Aharony, N. (2011). Librarians' attitudes toward knowledge management. *College & Research Libraries*, *72*(2), 111–126.

Aina, A. J., et al. (2011). Poor reading habits among Nigerians: the role of libraries. *Library Philosophy and Practice*. Retrieved from http://digitalcommons.unl.edu/libphilprac/529/.

Ajayi, L. (2011). A multiliteracies pedagogy: exploring semiotic possibilities of a Disney video in a third grade diverse classroom. *Urban Review*, *43*(3), 396–413.

Alansari, H. A. (2013). Public relations in academic libraries in Gulf Cooperation Council (GCC) states. *Library Management*, *34*(1/2), 68–82. http://dx.doi.org/10.1108/01435121311298289.

Alire, C. A. (2007). Word-of-mouth marketing: abandoning the academic library ivory tower. *New Library World*, *108*(11/12), 545–551. http://dx.doi.org/10.1108/03074800710838272.

American Library Association (ALA). (2008). *American library association code of ethics. Adopted by the ALA Council.*

American Library Association. (2000). *Information literacy competency standards for higher education.*

American Library Association. (2012). *Assessment in action: Academic libraries and student success.* Retrieved from http://www.ala.org/acrl/AiA.

Anderson, L. W. (2005). Objectives, evaluation, and the improvement of education. *Studies in Educational Evaluation*, *31*(2/3), 102–112. http://dx.doi.org/10.1016/j.stueduc2005.05.004.

Angel, C. M. (2011). Gap analysis of the University of South Carolina's digital collections department. *OCLC Systems & Services*, *27*(2), 99–112. http://dx.doi.org/10.1108/10650751111135409.

Arshad, A., & Ameen, K. (2010). Service quality of the University of the Punjab's libraries: an exploration of users' perceptions. *Performance Measurement and Metrics*, *11*(3), 313–325.

Ashcroft, L. (2004). Developing competencies, critical analysis and personal transferable skills in future information professionals. *Library Review*, *53*(2), 82–88.

Association of College and Research Libraries (ACRL). (2000). *Information literacy competency standards for higher education.* Retrieved April 16, 2010 from www.ala.org/ala/mgrps/divs/acrl/standards/informationliteracycompetency.cfm.

Association of College and Research Libraries Research Planning and Review Committee. (2012). 2012 top ten trends in academic libraries: a review of the trends and issues affecting academic libraries in higher education. *College & Research Libraries News*, *73*(6), 311–320.

Association of Research Libraries. (2012). *Issue brief: 21st-century collections: Calibration of investment and collaborative action.* Retrieved from http://www.arl.org/bm~doc/21stctfreport_11may12.pdf.

Averweg, U. R., & Leaning, M. A. (2011). Visions of community: community informatics and the contested nature of a polysemic term for a progressive discipline. *Information Technologies & International Development*, 7(2), 17–30.

Aydelott, K. (2007). Using the ACRL information literacy competency standards for science and engineering/technology to develop a modular critical-thinking-based information literacy tutorial. *Science & Technology Libraries*, 27(4), 19–42.

Ayo-Sobowale, M., & Akinyemi, S. (2011). Funding strategies for quality university education in Nigeria: the principle of fiscal justice. *Journal of Studies in Education*, 1(1). Retrieved from http://www.macrothink.org/journal/index.php/jse/article/view/1031/823.

Ayu, A., & Abrizah, A. A. (2011). Do you facebook? Usage and applications of facebook page among academic libraries in Malaysia. *International Information & Library Review*, 43(4), 239–249. http://dx.doi.org/10.1016/j.iilr.2011.10.005.

Baker, L. (2006). Library instruction in the rearview mirror: a reflective look at the evolution of a first-year library program using evidence-based practice. *College & Undergraduate Libraries*, 13(2), 1–12.

Bates, M. J. (2005). Information and knowledge: an evolutionary framework for information science. *Information Research*, 10(4), 10–14.

Bayley, L., Ferrell, S., & Mckinnell, J. (2009). Practicing what we preach: a case study on the application of evidence-based practice to inform decision making for public services staffing in an academic health sciences library. *New Review of Academic Librarianship*, 15(2), 235–252. http://dx.doi.org/10.1080/13614530903245311.

Bean, J., & Eaton, S. B. (2001). The psychology underlying successful retention practices. *Journal of College Student Retention*, 3(1), 73–89.

Beder, S. (1997). *Addressing the issues of social and academic integration for first year students: A discussion paper*. UltiBASE, RMIT. http://ultibase.mit.edu.au/Articles/dec97/beder1.htm.

Begum, S., & Siraj, N. (2003). Total quality management in the academic library. *Library Philosophy and Practice*, 5(2).

Begum, S. (2005). Total quality management in the academic library. *Library Philosophy and Practice (e-journal)*, 3.

Belkin, N. (1997). *A Concept of information for information science*. London: University of London.

Benjamin, R. (2008). The case for comparative institutional assessment of higher-order thinking skills. *Change: The Magazine of Higher Learning*, 40(6), 50–55.

Berger, P. (2006). More on digital literacy. *Information Searcher*, 16(4), 2.

Bierman, F. (2000). The case for a world environment organization. *Environment: Science and Policy for Sustainable Development*, 42(9), 22–31.

Birdsall, D. G. (1997). *Strategic planning in academic libraries: a political perspective. Restructuring Academic Libraries: Organizational Development in the Wake of Technological Change*.

Blake, L., & Ballance, D. (2013). Teaching evidence-based practice in the hospital and the library: two different groups, one course. *Medical Reference Services Quarterly*, 32(1), 100–110. http://dx.doi.org/10.1.1080/02763869.2013.749143.

Blummer, B., & Kenton, J. (2012). Best practices for integrating e-books in academic libraries: a literature review from 2005 to present. *Collection Management*, 37(2), 65–97. http://dx.doi.org/10.1080/01462679.2012.660851.

Bodi, S. (1988). Critical thinking and bibliographic instruction. *Journal of Academic Librarianship*, 14(3), 150.

Boekhorst, A. K. (2003). Becoming information literate in the Netherlands. *Library Review*, 52(7), 298–309.

Booth, A. (2006). Clear and present questions: formulating questions for evidence based practice. *Library Hi Tech*, 24(3), 355–368.

Borup Larsen, J., Kajberg, L., & LØrring, L. (2005). *A survey of library & information science schools in Europe. European curriculum reflections on Library and Information Science Education*. Copenhagen: Royal School of Library and Information Science, 232–242.

Boud, D. (2000). Sustainable assessment: rethinking assessment for the learning society. *Studies in continuing education, 22*(2), 151–167.

Breakstone, E. R. (2010). Now how much of your print collection is really online? an analysis of the overlap of print and digital holdings at the University of Oregon Law Library. *Legal Reference Services Quarterly, 29*(4), 255–275. http://dx.doi.org/10.1080/02703 19X.2010.527781.

Breeding, M. (2012). Coping with complex collections: managing print and digital. *Computers in Libraries, 32*(7), 23–26.

Breitbach, B., Tracey, R., & Neely, T. (2002). Managing a digital collection: the Garst photographic collection. *Reference Services Review, 30*(2), 124–142.

Brenner, M., Larsen, T., & Weston, C. (2006). Digital collection management through the library catalog. *Information Technology & Libraries, 25*(2), 65–77.

Brierton, S. (2012). Higher order thinking skills as demonstrated in synchronous and asynchronous online college discussion posts. *Dissertation Abstracts International Section A, 73*.

Brown, D., & Sen, B. (2010). The undergraduate prospectus as a marketing tool for academic libraries. *New Review of Academic Librarianship, 16*(2), 160–191. http://dx.doi.org/ 10.1080/13614531003791725.

Bruce, C., & Candy, P. (2000). *Information literacy around the world*. Wagga Wagga, Australia: Centre for Information Studies Charles Sturt University.

Budd, J. (2005). *The changing academic library: Operations, culture, environments* (No. 56). Association of College & Research Libraries.

Budd, J. M. (1998). *The academic library: Its context, its purpose, and its operation*. Englewood, CO: Libraries Unlimited.

Cain, A. (2002). Archimedes, reading, and the sustenance of academic research culture in library instruction. *Journal of Academic Librarianship, 28*(3), 115–121.

Campbell, J. D. (2006). Changing a cultural icon: the academic library as a virtual destination. *EDUCAUSE Review, 41*(1), 16–30.

Campello, B., & Abreu, V. L. F.G. (2005). Information literacy and the education of school librarians. *School Libraries Worldwide, 11*(1), 37–52.

Cannady, R. E., King, S. B., & Blendinger, J. G. (2012). Proactive outreach to adult students: a department and library collaborative effort. *Reference Librarian, 53*(2), 156–169. http://dx.doi.org/10.1080/0276. 3877.2011.608603.

Carlson, S., & Young, J. R. (2005). *Google will digitize and search millions of books from 5 top research libraries*. Chronicle of Higher Education, A37–A40.

Carr, P. L., & Collins, M. D. D. (Eds.). (2008). *Managing the transition from print to electronic journals and resources: A guide for library and information professionals*. New York: Routledge.

Carr, D. (2003). *Information professions*. London: Routledge.

Carter, T. M., & Seaman, P. (2011). The management and support of outreach in academic libraries. *Reference & User Services Quarterly, 51*(2), 163–171.

Castiglione, J. (2008). Facilitating employee creativity in the library environment: an important managerial concern for library administrators. *Library Management, 29*(3), 159–172.

Chadwell, F. A. (2011). What's next for collection management and managers? *Collection Management, 36*(4), 198–202. http://dx.doi.org/10.1080/01462679.2011.607555.

Chan, C. (2012). Marketing the academic library with online social network advertising. *Library Management, 33*(8/9), 479–489. http://dx.doi.org/10.1108/01435121211279849.

Chartered Institute of Information and Library Professionals (CILIP). (2006). *A short introduction to information literacy*. http://www.cilip.org.uk/policyadvocacy/learning/informa tionliteracy/definition/introduction.htm.

Chen, M., & Reilly, M. (2011). Implementing METS, MIX, and DC for sustaining digital preservation at the University of Houston libraries. *Journal of Library Metadata, 11*(2), 83–99. http://dx.doi.org/10.1080/19386389.2011.570662.

Cody, D. E. (2006). Critical thoughts on critical thinking. *Journal of Academic Librarianship*, *32*(4), 402–403.

Collins, M. (2009). Evolving workflows: knowing when to hold'em, knowing when to fold'em. *Serials Librarian*, *57*(3), 261–271. http://dx.doi.org/10.1080/03615260902877050.

Connaway, L. S., & Dickey, T. J. (2010). *The digital information seeker: Report of the findings from select OCLC, RIN, and JISC user behavior projects*.

Conway, P. (2008). Modeling the digital content landscape in universities. *Library Hi Tech*, *26*(3), 342–354.

Cooke, L., Norris, M., Busby, N., Page, T., Franklin, G., Gadd, E., et al. (2011). Evaluating the impact of academic liaison librarians on their user community: a review and case study. *New Review of Academic Librarianship*, *17*(1), 5–30.

Cousins, J., & Ross, J. A. (1993). Improving higher order thinking skills by teaching 'with' the computer: a comparative study. *Journal of Research on Computing in Education*, *26*(1), 94.

Coyle, K. (2006). Technology and the return on investment. *Journal of Academic Librarianship*, *32*(5), 537–539.

Cross, R. L. (2010). Economic principles and across-the-board cuts. *The Bottom Line*, *23*(4), 227–231.

Crowley, B. (2008). Lifecycle librarianship. *Library Journal*, *133*(6), 46.

Crowley, W. A. (2008). *Renewing professional librarianship: A fundamental rethinking*. Libraries Unltd Incorporated.

Cummings, L. (2007). Bursting out of the box: outreach to the millennial generation through student services programs. *Reference Services Review*, *35*(2), 285–295. http://dx.doi.org/10.1108/00907320710749191.

Dearing, R. (1997). *The national committee of inquiry into higher education*. A summary report. Norwich: HMSO.

Demas, S., & Miller, M. (2012). Curating collective collections — what's your plan? Writing collection management plans. *Against The Grain*, *24*(1), 65–68.

Dennis, M. (2012). Outreach initiatives in academic libraries, 2009–2011. *Reference Services Review*, *40*(3), 368–383. http://dx.doi.org/10.1108/00907321211254643.

DeVoe, K. (2006). Collection assessment in the digital age. *Against The Grain*, *18*(5), 1–18.

Dillon, A. (2007). LIS as a research domain: problems and prospects. *Information Research*, *12*(4), 12–14.

Duke, L. M., & Tucker, T. (2007). How to develop a marketing plan for an academic library. *Technical Services Quarterly*, *25*(1), 51. http://dx.doi.org/10.1300/J124v25n01•05.

Duke, L. M., MacDonald, J. B., & Trimble, C. S. (2009). Collaboration between marketing students and the library: an experiential learning project to promote reference services. *College & Research Libraries*, *70*(2), 109–121.

Dunn, R., & Menchaca, F. (2009). The present is another country: academic libraries, learning technologies, and relevance. *Journal of Library Administration*, *49*(5), 469–479.

Edwards, R. G., & Williams, C. J. (1998). Performance appraisal in academic libraries: minor changes or major renovation? *Library Review*, *47*(1), 14–19.

Eldredge, J. (2006). Evidence-based librarianship: the EBL process. *Library Hi Tech*, *24*(3), 341–354.

Ellis, E. L., & Whatley, K. M. (2008). The evolution of critical thinking skills in library instruction, 1986–2006: a selected and annotated bibliography and review of selected programs. *College & Undergraduate Libraries*, *15*(1/2), 5–20. http://dx.doi.org/10.1080/10691310802176665.

Elmborg, J. (2006). Critical information literacy: implications for instructional practice. *The Journal of Academic Librarianship*, *32*(2), 192–199.

Emmons, M., & Wilkinson, F. C. (2010). The academic library impact on student persistence. *College & Research Libraries* crl-74rt.

Empey, H., & Black, N. E. (2005). Marketing the academic library: building on the "@ your library" framework. *College & Undergraduate Libraries*, *12*(1/2), 19–33. http://dx.doi.org/10.1300/J106v12n01–02.

Estall, C., & Stephens, D. (2011). A study of the variables influencing academic library staff's attitudes toward marketing. *New Review of Academic Librarianship, 17*(2), 185–208. http://dx.doi.org/10.1080/13614533.2011.610217.

Farmer, L. J. (2009). The life cycle of digital reference sources. *Reference Librarian, 50*(2), 117–136. http://dx.doi.org/10.1080/02763870902755957.

Feeney, M. M. (1999). *Digital culture: Maximising the nation's investment: A synthesis of JISC/NPO studies on the preservation of electronic materials.* London: National Preservation Office.

Fernandez, L., & Nariani, R. (2011). Open access funds: a Canadian library survey. *Partnership: The Canadian Journal of Library and Information Practice and Research, 6*(1).

Fisher, B. (2004). Workforce skills development: the professional imperative for information services in the United Kingdom. Paper presented at the ALIA Biennial Conference, Gold Coast, Australia. Retrieved from http://conferences.alia.org.au/alia2004/pdfs/fisher.b.paper.pdf.

Flatley, R. K., & Prock, K. (2009). E-Resource collection development: a survey of current practices in academic libraries. *Library Philosophy & Practice, 11*(2), 1–4.

Fletcher, C. H., Flahive, R., Ford, E., & Fletcher, R. (2010). Integrating Bloom's taxonomy of critical thinking with physical geology content. *Abstracts with Programs – Geological Society of America, 42*(5), 189.

Fletcher, C. H., Flahive, R., Ford, E., & Fletcher, R. (November 2010). Integrating Bloom's taxonomy of critical thinking with physical geology content. In *2010 GSA Denver Annual Meeting.*

Foo, S., Chaudhry, A. S., Majid, S. M., & Logan, E. (2002). Academic libraries in transition: challenges ahead. In *Proceedings of the world Library summit, keynote address: Academic Library Seminar.* Singapore: National Library Board. April 22–26.

Foster, M., Wilson, H., Allensworth, N., & Sands, D. T. (2010). Marketing research guides: an online experiment with LibGuides. *Journal of Library Administration, 50*(5/6), 602–616. http://dx.doi.org/10.1080/01930826.2010.488922.

Foster, A. E. (2006). Information literacy for the information profession: experiences from Aberystwyth. Paper presented at the Aslib proceedings.

Foulonneau, M., Cole, T. W., Blair, C., Gorman, P. C., Hagedorn, K., & Riley, J. (2006). The CIC metadata portal: a collaborative effort in the area of digital libraries. *Science & Technology Libraries, 26*(3/4), 111–135. http://dx.doi.org/10.1.300/J I 22v26n0308.

Fourie, I., & Ball, L. (2012). Promotional strategies for information products and services: aligning with the serious and entertainment facets of information consumers' lives. *Library Hi Tech, 30*(4), 683–692. http://dx.doi.org/10.1108/07378831211285130.

Fourie, I. (2004). Librarians and the claiming of new roles: how can we try to make a difference? Paper presented at the Aslib proceedings.

Fowler, R. K. (1998). The university library as learning organization for innovation: an exploratory study. *College and Research Libraries, 59*(3).

Framework for good digital collections: Version 3 Released by NISO, IMLS. *Library Hi Tech News, 25*(2/3), (2008), 19–20.

Freire, P. (1970). *Pedagogy of the oppressed.* New York: Continuum.

Frumkin, J., & Reese, T. (2011). Provision recognition: increasing awareness of the library's value in delivering electronic information resources. *Journal of Library Administration, 51*(7/8), 810–819. http://dx.doi.org/10.1080/01930826.2011.601277.

Galston, C., Huber, E. K., Johnson, K., & Long, A. (2012). Community reference: making libraries indispensable in a new way. *American Libraries, 43*(5/6), 46–50.

Gannon-Leary, P. (2006). Glut of information, death of knowledge? A consideration of the information needs of practitioners identified during the FAME project. *Library Review, 55*(2), 120–131.

Gerke, J., & Maness, J. M. (2010). The physical and the virtual: the relationship between library as place and electronic collections. *College & Research Libraries, 71*(1), 20–31.

Germano, M. A. (2010). Narrative-based library marketing: selling your library's value during tough economic times. *Bottom Line: Managing Library Finances, 23*(1), 5–17. http://dx.doi.org/10.1108/08880451011049641.

Gerolimos, M., & Konsta, R. (2008). Librarians' skills and qualifications in a modern informational environment. *Library Management, 29*(8/9), 691–699.

Gerolimos, M. (2009). Skills developed through library and information science education. *Library Review, 58*(7), 527–540.

Giesecke, J., & McNeil, B. (2004). Transitioning to the learning organization. *Library Trends, 53*(1). Retrieved from https://www.ideals.illinois.edu/bitstream/handle/2142/1031/LT-53-1.pdf.

Gilbert, J. K. (2009). Using assessment data to investigate library instruction for first year students. *Communications in Information Literacy, 3*(2), 181–192.

Glynn, L. (2006). A critical appraisal tool for library and information research. *Library Hi Tech, 24*(3), 387–399.

Goldman, B. (2011). Bridging the gap: taking practical steps toward managing born-digital collections in manuscript repositories. *RBM: A Journal of Rare Books, Manuscripts, & Cultural Heritage, 12*(1), 11–24.

Gómez, R., López, M., Prats, J., & Rovira, A. (2004). Towards the Integral Management of Library collections at the Technical University of Catalonia (UPC) *IATUL Annual Conference Proceedings 14*(1)

Goodfellow, R. (2011). Literacy, literacies, and the digital in higher education. *Teaching in Higher Education, 16*(1), 131–144.

Goodwin, I. (2007). Community Informatics and the local state in the UK: Facilitating or assimilating an agenda for change? *Information, Communication & Society, 10*(2), 194–218. http://dx.doi.org/10.1080/13691180701307446.

Gorman, M. (2003). *Whither library education? Keynote speech at the joint EUCLID/ALISE conference.* Paper presented at the EUCLID/ALISE Conference.

Goulding, A. (2001). Information poverty or overload? *Journal of Librarianship and Information Science, 33*(3), 109–111.

Greenwood, H., & Cleeve, M. (2008). Embracing change: evidence-based librarianship: the EBL process. *Library Management, 29*(3), 173–184.

Gregory, J. M., Weber, A. I., & Dippie, S. R. (2008). Innovative roles for technical services librarians: extending our reach. *Technical Services Quarterly, 25*(4), 37–47.

Grzeschik, K. (2010). Return on investment (ROI) in German libraries: the Berlin school of library and information science and the university library at the Humboldt University, Berlin – a case study. *The Bottom Line, 23*(4), 141–201.

Gueguen, G., & Hanlon, A. M. (2009). A collaborative workflow for the digitization of unique materials. *Journal of Academic Librarianship, 35*(5), 468–474.

Harris, L. (2010). *Academic libraries and student retention* OLA Conference University of Michigan. Powerpoint PPT presentation. Retrieved from SlideServe . http://www.slideserve.com/paul2/academic-libraries-student-retention.

Harris, V. A., & Weller, A. C. (2012). Use of special collections as an opportunity for outreach in the academic library. *Journal of Library Administration, 52*(3/4), 294–303. http://dx.doi.org/10.1080/01930826.2012.684508.

Hazen, D. (2011). Lost in the cloud: research library collections and community in the digital age. In *Association for Library Collections and Technical Services* (55). ALCTS.

Hebrang Grgić, I., & Špiranec, S. (2013). Information literacy of LIS students at the University of Zagreb: pros or just average millenials. Presented in European Conference on Information Literacy, October 2013.

Henry, C. L., Vardeman, K. K., & Syma, C. K. (2012). Reaching out: connecting students to their personal librarian. *Reference Services Review, 40*(3), 396–407.

Hernon, P., & Rossiter, N. (2006). Emotional intelligence: which traits are most prized? *College & Research Libraries, 67*(3), 260–275.

Hills, J. A. (2004). Better teaching with Deming and Bloom. *Quality Progress, 37*(3), 57–64.

Hjørland, B. (2000). Library and information science: practice, theory, and philosophical basis. *Information Processing & Management, 36*(3), 501–531.

Hopson, M. H., Simms, R. L., & Knezek, G. A. (2001). Using a technology-enriched environment to improve higher-order thinking skills. *Journal of Research on Technology in Education, 34*(2), 109–120.

Horava, T. (2010a). Challenges and possibilities for collection management in a digital age. *Library Resources & Technical Services, 54*(3), 142–152.

Horava, T. (2010b). Collection management and sustainability in the digital age: chasing the Holy grail. *Against The Grain, 22*(6), 22–26.

Horváth, T. (1999). A könyvtártudomány és információtudomány alapjai. (The basics of library science and information science [In Hungarian]). In T. Horváth, & I. Papp (Eds.), *Könyvtárosok kézikönyve. 1. Alapvetés* (pp. *18–75*). Budapest: Osiris.

Hubbard, S. (2001). The art of managing digital collections at the Getty Research Institute. *NFAIS Newsletter, 43*(12), 150–151.

Hurford, A. A., & Runyon, C. F. (2011). New workflows for born-digital assets: managing Charles E. Bracker's Orchid photographs collection. *Computers in Libraries, 31*(1), 6.

Hutton, J. (2008). Academic libraries as digital gateways: Linking students to the burgeoning wealth of open online collections. *Journal of Library Administration, 48*(3/4), 495–507.

Huwe, T. K. (2010). Building digital libraries. Hearts, minds, and the library's physical space. *Computers in Libraries, 30*(8), 29–31.

Huwe, T. K. (2011). Building digital libraries. HathiTrust's ascendance as a web-level digital library. *Computers in Libraries, 31*(8), 32–34.

Igwe, K. N. (2011). Reading culture and Nigeria's quest for sustainable development. *Library Philosophy and Practice.* Retrieved from http://digitalcommons.unl.edu/libphilprac/482/.

IMLS grants to support ROI study, digitization, more. *Library Journal, 134*(17), (2009), 14.

Jamali, R., Moshabaki, A., Aramoon, H., & Alimohammadi, A. (2013). Customer relationship management in electronic environment. *Electronic Library, 31*(1), 119–130. http://dx.doi.org/10.1108/02640471311299173.

James-Gilboe, L. (2010). Raising the library profile to fight budget challenges. *Serials Librarian, 59*(3/4), 360–369. http://dx.doi.org/10.1080/03615261003623112.

Jayasundara, C., Ngulube, P., & Minishi-Majanja, M. K. (2009). A theoretical model to predict customer satisfaction in relation to service quality in selected university libraries in Sri Lanka. *South African Journal of Libraries & Information Science, 75*(2), 179–194.

Jeng, J. (2005). What is usability in the context of the digital library and how can it be measured? *Information Technology & Libraries, 24*(2), 47–56.

Jin, T., & Bouthillier, F. (2012). The Integration of intelligence analysis into LIS education. *Journal of Education for Library and Information Science, 53*(2), 130–148.

Johns, C. (2003). Collection management strategies in a digital environment. *Collection Management, 28*(1/2), 37–43. http://dx.doi.org/10.1300/J105v28n01_04.

Johnson, J., & Mandity, E. (2010). Real challenges to virtual reality: realizing your collection through digital partnership. *Computers in Libraries, 30*(9), 18–22.

Johnson, C. M., Lindsay, E., & Water, S. (2008). Learning more about how they think: information literacy instruction in a campus-wide critical thinking project. *College & Undergraduate Libraries, 15*(1/2), 231–254.

Johnston, B., & Webber, S. (2004). The role of LIS faculty in the information literate university: taking over the academy? *New Library World, 105*(1/2), 12–20.

Jones, D., McCandless, M., Kiblinger, K., Giles, K., & McCabe, J. (2011). Simple marketing techniques and space planning to increase circulation. *Collection Management, 36*(2), 107–118. http://dx.doi.org/10.1080/01462679.2011.553774.

Jordan, J. (2010). Climbing out of the box and into the cloud: building web-scale for libraries. *Journal of Library Administration, 51*(1), 3–17.

Juznic, P., & Urbanija, J. (2003). Developing research skills in library and information science studies. *Library Management, 24*(6/7), 324–331.

Kaba, A. (2011). Marketing information resources and services on the web: current status of academic libraries in the United Arab Emirates. *Information Development, 27*(1), 58–65. http://dx.doi.org/10.1177/0266666910394625.

Kaur, K. (2009). Marketing the academic library on the web. *Library Management, 30*(6), 454–468. http://dx.doi.org/10.1108/01435120910982140.

Kellner, D. (1998). Multiple literacies and critical pedagogy in a multicultural society. *Educational Theory, 48*, 102–122.

Kelly, M. C., & Kross, A. (Eds.). (2002). *Making the grade: Academic libraries and student success.* Chicago: American Library Association.

Khoo, C. (2005). Competencies for new era librarians and information professionals. Paper presented at the International Conference on Libraries (ICOL 2005), March 14–16, 2005, Penang, Malaysia.

Kichuk, D. (2010). Electronic collection growth: an academic library case study. *Collection Building, 29*(2), 55–64.

Kirton, J., Barham, L., & Brady, S. (2008). Understanding and practice of information literacy in Australian government libraries. *Australian Library Journal, 57*(3), 237–256.

Koltay, T. (2007). A new direction for library and information science: the communication aspect of information literacy. *Information Research, 12*.

Koufogiannakis, D., & Crumley, E. (2006). Research in librararianship: issues to consider. *Library Hi Tech, 24*(3), 324–340. http://dx.doi.org/10.1108/07378830610692109.

Krathwoh, D. R. (2002). A revision of Bloom's taxonomy: an overview. *Theory Into Practice, 41*(4), 212–218.

Kreitz, P. A. (2009). Leadership and emotional intelligence: a study of university library directors and their senior management teams. *College & Research Libraries, 70*(6), 531–554.

Kretzschmar, W. A., & Potter, W. G. (2010). Library collaboration with large digital humanities projects. *Literary & Linguistic Computing, 25*(4), 439–445. http://dx.doi.org/10.1093/llc/fqq022.

Kuh, G. D., & Gonyea, R. M. (2003). The role of the academic library in promoting student engagement in learning. *College & Research Libraries, 64*(4), 256–282.

Kuhlthau, C. C. (1993). A principle of uncertainty for information seeking. *Journal of Documentation, 49*(4), 339–355.

Kulp, C., & Rupp-Serrano, K. (2005). Organizational approaches to electronic resource acquisition: decision-making models in libraries. *Collection Management, 30*(4), 3–29.

Lampert, C., & Vaughan, J. (2009). Success factors and strategic planning: rebuilding an academic library digitization program. *Information Technology & Libraries, 28*(3), 116–136.

Lewis, D. W. (2007). A strategy for academic libraries in the first quarter of the 21st century. *College & Research Libraries, 68*(5), 418–434.

Libraries of the Future. (2012). *Sponsored by the British Library, JISC, the Research Information Network (RIN), Research Libraries UK (RLUK) and the society of college.* National and University Libraries (SCONUL). Retrieved from http://www.futurelibraries.info/content/.

Lindsay, J., Kemper, A., & Oelschlegel, S. (2012). Evaluating print collections for a transition to digital. *Journal of Electronic Resources in Medical Libraries, 9*(1), 35–46. http://dx.doi.org/10.1080/15424065.2011.651572.

Line, M. B. (2005). Librarianship as it is practiced: a failure of intellect, imagination and initiative. *Interlending and Document Supply, 33*(2), 109–133.

Lone, F. A. (2011). Reading habits of rural and urban college students in the 21st century. *Library Philosophy and Practice.* Retrieved from http://unllib.unl.edu/LPP/lone.htm.

Lopatin, L. (2010). Metadata practices in academic and non-academic libraries for digital projects: a survey. *Cataloging & Classification Quarterly, 48*(8), 716–742. http://dx.doi.org/10.1080/01639374.2010.509029.

Lorenzen, M. (2010). Fund raising for academic libraries: what works, what doesn't? *Library Philosophy & Practice, 12*(2), 1–21.

Lowry, C. B. (2005). Let's call it the "ubiquitous library" instead. *portal: Libraries and the Academy, 5*(3), 293–296.

Lupton, M. (2008). *Information literacy and learning: Blackwood.* South Australia: Auslib Press.

Ma, A. W. (2009). Computer supported collaborative learning and higher order thinking skills: a case study of textile studies. *Interdisciplinary Journal of E-Learning & Learning Objects,* 5145–5167.

MacDonald, K. I., Van Duinkerken, W., & Stephens, J. (2008). It's all in the marketing: the impact of a virtual reference marketing campaign at Texas A&M University. *Reference & User Services Quarterly, 47*(4), 375–385.

Macdonald, J. (2004). Developing competent e-learners: the role of assessment. *Assessment & Evaluation in Higher Education, 29*(2), 215–226.

Madhuri, G. V., Kantamreddi, V., & Goteli, P. (2012). Promoting higher order thinking skills using inquiry-based learning. *European Journal of Engineering Education, 37*(3), 117–123.

Madhuri, G. V., Kantamreddi, V. S. S.N., & Prakash Goteti, L. N. S. (2012). Promoting higher order thinking skills using inquiry-based learning. *European Journal of Engineering Education, 37*(2), 117–123.

Maloney, K., Antelman, K., Arlitsch, K., & Butler, J. (2010). Future leaders' views on organizational culture. *College & Research Libraries* crl-47.

Maloney, M. M. (2012). Cultivating community, promoting inclusivity: collections as fulcrum for targeted outreach. *New Library World, 113*(5/6), 281–289. http://dx.doi.org/10.1108/03074801211226364.

Marketing electronic resources to distance students. (2007). A multipronged approach. *Serials Librarian, 53*(3), 77–93.

Marlow, L., & Inman, D. (1992). Higher order thinking skills: teachers' perceptions. *Education, 112*(4), 538.

Martin, C. (2012). One-minute video: marketing your library to faculty. *Reference Services Review, 40*(4), 589–600. http://dx.doi.org/10.1108/00907321211277387.

Mathson, S. M., & Lorenzen, M. G. (2008). We won't be fooled again: teaching critical thinking via evaluation of hoax and historical revisionist websites in a library credit course. *College & Undergraduate Libraries, 15*(1–2), 211–230.

Matthews, B. S. (2009). Marketing today's academic library: a bold new approach to communicating with students. *American Library Association.*

Maxey-Harris, C. (2010). Multicultural e-resources: an exploratory study of resources held by ARL libraries. *Behavioral & Social Sciences Librarian, 29*(1), 65–80. http://dx.doi.org/10.1080/01639260903571880.

Mayer, R. E. (2002). A taxonomy for computer-based assessment of problem solving. *Computers in Human Behavior, 18*(6), 623–632.

Mays, R., Tenopir, C., & Kaufman, P. (2010). Lib-Value: Measuring value and return on investment of academic libraries. *Research Library Issues, 271,* 36–40.

McGuigan, G. S. (2012). Addressing change in academic libraries: a review of classica-908 qwe45rt7890-rganizational theory and implications for academic libraries. *Library Philosophy and Practice.* Retrieved from http://digitalcommons.unl.edu/cgi/viewcontent.cgi?article=1829&context=libphilprac.

Mee, S. (2013). Outreach to international campuses: removing barriers and building relationships. *Journal of Library & Information Services in Distance Learning, 7*(1/2), 1–17. http://dx.doi.org/10.1080/1533290X.2012.705173.

Menchaca, F. (2012). The future is in doubt: librarians, publishers, and networking learning in the 21st Century. *Journal of Library Administration, 52*(5), 396–410. http://dx.doi.org/10.1080/01930826.2012.700804.

Milewisicz, E. J. (2009). *"But is it a library?" The contested meanings and changing culture of the academic library* Doctoral Dissertation. Retrieved from Emory University Electronic Thesis and Dissertation Repository . http://pid.emory.edu/ark:/25593/1981m.

Milewicz, E. J. (2009). Origin and development of the information commons in academic libraries. *A field guide to the information commons,* 3–17.

Miller, C. (2011). Creating intelligent libraries. *Information Outlook, 15*(4), 27–29.

Milner-Bolotin, M., & Nashon, S. (2012). The essence of student visual-spatial literacy and higher order thinking skills in undergraduate biology. *Protoplasma, 249*(Suppl. 1), S25–S30.

Mintzberg, H. (1990). The manager's job: Folklore and fact. *Harvard Business Review, March–April,* 163–167.

Missingham, R. (2006). Library and information science: skills for twenty-first century professionals. *Library Management, 27*(4/5), 257–268.

Molesworth, M., Nixon, E., & Scullion, R. (2009). Having, being and higher education: the Marketization of the university and the transformation of the student into consumer. *Teaching in higher Education, 14*(3), 277–287 345678.

Montiel-Overall, P. (2009). Cultural competence: a conceptual framework for library and information science professionals. *Library Quarterly, 79*(2), 175–204.

Moore, P. (2002). An analysis of information literacy education worldwide. White paper prepared for UNESCO, the US National Commission on libraries and information science, and the National Forum on Information Literacy. Paper presented at the information literacy meeting of experts, Prague, the Czech Republic, July 2002.

Moran, J. F. (2008). So much more power that we think we have. *Library Administration & Management,* 42–43.

Morellion, J., Luhala, M., & Russo, C. T. (2011). Learning that sticks: engaged educators + engaged learners. *School Library Monthly, 28*(1), 17–20.

Morrell, E. (2012). 21st-century literacies, critical media pedagogies, and language arts. *Reading Teacher, 66*(4), 300–302.

Mortimore, J. M. (2006). Access-informed collection development and the academic library: using holdings, circulation, and ILL data to develop prescient collections. *Collection Management, 30*(3), 21–37.

Mu, C. (2007). Marketing academic library resources and information services to international students from Asia. *Reference Services Review, 35*(4), 571–583.

Mundava, M. C., & Gray, L. (2008). Meeting them where they are: marketing to international student populations in US academic libraries. *Technical Services Quarterly, 25*(3), 35–48.

Narayanan, S., & Adithan, M. M. (2012). Developing a new teaching approach for training of engineering faculty in higher order thinking skills (HOTS). *Proceedings of the West Virginia Academy of Science, 83*(2), 1–7.

National Committee of Inquiry into Higher Education Summary Report. (1997). *Cambridge university reporter, 8th October 1997. The chancellor, masters and schools of the University of Cambridge.*

Nazim, M., & Mukherjee, B. (2011). Status of institutional repositories in Asian countries: a quantitative study. *Library Philosophy and Practice.* Retrieved from http://unllib.unl.edu/LPP/nazim-mukherjee.htm.

Nelson, N. L. (2012). Managing born-digital special collections and archival materials. In *SPEC kit, 329.* Washington, DC: Association of Research Libraries.

Nichols, T. (2010). Ensuring higher order thinking skills development in distance learning. *Distance Learning, 7*(3), 69–71.

Nikolaidou, M., Anagnostopoulos, D., & Hatzopoulos, M. (2005). Development of a medical digital library managing multiple collections. *Electronic Library, 23*(2), 221–236. http://dx.doi.org/10.1108/02640470510592933.

NISO Framework Working Group with support from the Institute of Museum and Library Services. (2007). *A framework for building good digital collections* (3ʳᵈ edition). . Available from. http://www.niso.org/publications/rp/framework3.pdf.

Nunn, B., & Ruane, E. (2011). Marketing gets personal: promoting reference staff to reach users. *Journal of Library Administration, 51*(3), 291–300. http://dx.doi.org/10.1080/01930 826.2011.556945.

Nwezeh, C. T. (2010). Public relations in Nigerian university libraries: the case of Hezekiah Oluwasanmi library. *Obafemi Awolowo University. Electronic Library, 28*(1), 100–107.

Oakleaf, M. (2009). The information literacy instruction assessment cycle: a guide for increasing student learning and improving librarian instructional skills. *Journal of Documentation, 65*(4), 539–560.

O'Connor, L., & Lundstrom, K. (2011). The impact of social marketing strategies on the information seeking behaviors of college students. *Reference & User Services Quarterly, 50*(4), 351–365.

Oder, N., Blumenstein, L., Hadro, J., Rapp, D., & Zisko, A. (2010). New studies measure academic library ROI. *Library Journal, 135*(15), 13.

Odlyzko, A. (1997). The economics of electronic journals. *First Monday, 2*(8–4) August 1997.

Oehlerts, B., & Liu, S. (2013). Digital preservation strategies at Colorado State University libraries. *Library Management, 34*(1/2), 83–95. http://dx.doi.org/10.1108/ 01435121311298298.

Okoye, M. O., & Ejikeme, A. N. (2011). Open access, institutional repositories, and scholarly publishing: the role of librarians in South Eastern Nigeria. *Library Philosophy and Practice.* Retrieved from http://unllib.unl.edu/LPP/okoye-ejikeme.htm.

Oliver, D., & Dobele, T. (2007). First year courses in it: a Bloom Rating. *Journal of Information Technology Education, 6,* 347–360.

Parirokh, M. (2008). *Information literacy education: Concepts, methods, applications.* Tehran: Ketabdar.

Pascarella, J. (2008). Confronting the challenges of critical digital literacy: an essay review critical constructivism. *A primer. Educational Studies, 43*(3), 246–255.

Pashler, H., McDaniel, M., Rohrer, D., & Bjork, R. (2008). Learning styles: Concepts and evidence. *Psychological Science in the Public Interest, 9,* 105–119.

Pedley, P. (2001). The information professional of the 21st century. *Managing Information, 8*(7), 8–9.

Pena, C., & Almaguer, I. (2012). The use of online discussions to foster critical thinking in a teacher education program. *International Journal of Instructional Media, 39*(1), 25–32.

Perrault, A. H., & Dixon, J. (2007). Collection assessment: the Florida community college experience. *Community & Junior College Libraries, 14*(1), 7–20.

Polly, D. (2011). Developing students' higher order thinking skills (HOTS) through technology-rich texts. *Educational Technology, 51*(4), 20–26.

Porter, B. (2010). Managing with emotional intelligence. *Library Leadership & Management, 24*(4), 199–201.

Powell, R. R. (1989). Problem solving in libraries: a festschrift in honor of Herbert Goldhor. *Library Trends, 38*(2), 153–325.

Prebor, G. (2010). Analysis of the interdisciplinary nature of library and information science. *Librarianship and Information Science, 42*(4), 256–267.

Price, A. C. (2009). How to make a dollar out of fifteen cents: Tips for electronic collection development. *Collection Building, 28*(1), 31–34.

Prilop, V., Westbrook, R. N., & German, E. (2012). Collaborative project development in the creation of an interdepartmental digitization workflow. *Collaborative Librarianship, 4*(2), 60–66.

Promis, P. (2008). Are employers asking for the right competencies? A case for emotional intelligence. *Library Administration & Management, 22*(1), 24–30.

Rafiq, M., & Ameen, K. (2013). Digitization in university libraries of Pakistan. *OCLC Systems & Services, 29*(1), 37–46. http://dx.doi.org/10.1108/10650751311294546.

Rahimi, G., & Damirchi, G. (2011). Surveying of relationship between multiple intelligences and critical thinking of Islamic Azad University managers in 13th region. *Interdisciplinary Journal of Contemporary Research in Business, 3*(2), 1093–1100.

Raju, R., & Raju, J. (2010). The public library as a critical institution in South Africa's democracy: a reflection. *Libres: Library and Information Science Research Electronic Journal, 20*(1). Available http://libres.curtin.edu.au/.

Rao, S., Cameron, A., & Gaskin-Noel, S. (2009). Embedding general education competencies into an online information literacy course. *Journal of Library Administration, 49*(1/2), 59–73. http://dx.doi.org/10.80/01930820802310858.

Rasch, L. (2004). Employee performance appraisal and the 95/5 rule. *Community College Journal of Research and Practice, 28*(5), 407–414.

Rentfrow, D. (2006). Thematic research collections and women's studies. *Women's Studies International Forum, 29*(3), 307–316. http://dx.doi.org/10.1016/j.wsif.2006.04.009.

Robinson, C. K. (2012). Peter Drucker on marketing: application and implications for libraries. *Bottom Line: Managing Library Finances, 25*(1), 4–12. http://dx.doi.org/10.1108/08880451211229153.

Rudin, P. (2008). No fixed address: the evolution of outreach library services on university campuses. *Reference Librarian, 49*(1), 55–75.

Rutten, K. (2011). Academic discourse and literacy narratives as "equipment for living." *CLCWeb: Comparative Literature & Culture: A WWWeb Journal, 13*(4), 1–9.

Sacchanand, C. (2000). Workplace learning for information professionals in a changing information environment. Paper presented at the 66th IFLA Council and General Conference, Jerusalem.

Safley, E. (2006). Designed to deliver: building a digital collection to support research. In *IATUL Annual Conference Proceedings* (16) (pp. 30–35).

Samson, S. (2010). Information literacy learning outcomes and student success. *Journal of Academic Librarianship, 36*(3), 202–210.

Saracevic, T. (1999). Information science. *Journal of the American Society for Information Science, 50*(12), 1051–1063.

Sarjeant-Jenkins, R. (2012). Why market? *Library Leadership & Management, 26*(1), 1–8.

Saunders, L. (2009). The future of academic libraries: a Delphi study. *Libraries and the Academy, 9*(1), 99–114.

Schonfeld, R. C. (2010). Managing our collections in a digital age. (cover story). *Against The Grain, 22*(5), 1–16.

Seeholzer, J. (2011). Charting a new course: a case study on the impact of outreach events at Kent State University Libraries. *Public Services Quarterly, 7*(3/4), 125–135. http://dx.doi.org/10.1080/15228959.2011.623595.

Seo and Zanish-Belcher, T (2006). Pitfalls, progress, and partnership: collaboration between special collections and preservation in academic libraries. *Collection Management, 30*(3), 3–19.

Shafique, F. (2009). Marketing research as a tool for finding library users' needs and demands: application of three party theory. *Library Philosophy & Practice, 11*(1), 1–7.

Sharman, A., & Walsh, A. (2012). Roving librarian at a mid-sized, UK-Based university. *Library Technology Reports, 48*(8), 28–34.

Sharp, K. (2001). Internet librarianship: traditional roles in a new environment. *IFLA Journal, 27*(2), 78–81.

Shearer, B. S., Klatt, C., & Nagy, S. P. (2009). Development of a new academic digital library: a study of usage data of a core medical electronic journal collection. *Journal of The Medical Library Association, 97*(2), 93–101.

Sheldon, D. A. (2005). Comparisons of higher-order thinking skills among prospective freshman and upper-level pre-service music education majors. *Journal of Research in Music Education, 53*(1), 40–50.

Shin, Y., & Shin, D. (2012). Community Informatics and the new urbanism: incorporating information and communication technologies into planning integrated urban communities. *Journal of Urban Technology, 19*(1), 23–42.

Sibbel, A. (2009). Pathways towards sustainability through higher education. *International Journal of Sustainability in Higher Education, 10*(1), 68–82.

Sidorko, P. (2010). Demonstrating RoI in the library: the holy grail search continues. *Library Management*, *31*(8), 645–653. http://dx.doi.org/10.1108/01435121011093414.

Singer, H., & Ruddell, R. B. (1985). *Theoretical models and the processes of reading* (3rd ed.). Newark, DE: International Reading Association.

Sinn, D. (2012). Impact of digital archival collections on historical research. *Journal of the American Society For Information Science & Technology*, *63*(8), 1521–1537. http://dx.doi.org/10.1002/asi.22650.

Skekel, D. (2008). Digital collections: Transforming the work of libraries. *Journal of Library Metadata*, *8*(2), 147–153. http://dx.doi.org/10.1080/10911360802087341.

Smith, D. (2006). Collection inventory in the digital age: how can we analyze until we know what we have? *Against The Grain*, *18*(5), 18–22.

Smith, D. A. (2011). Strategic marketing of library resources and services. *College & Undergraduate Libraries*, *18*(4), 333–349. http://dx.doi.org/10.1080/10691316.2011.624937.

Somerville, M. M., & Brar, N. (2009). A user-centered and evidence-based approach for digital library projects. *Electronic Library*, *27*(3), 409–425.

Southwell, K. L., & Slater, J. (2012). Accessibility of digital special collections using screen readers. *Library Hi Tech*, *30*(3), 457–471. http://dx.doi.org/10.1108/07378831211266609.

Sowell, S. L., Boock, M. H., Landis, L. A., & Nutefall, J. E. (2012). Between a rock and a hard place: managing government document collections in a digital world. *Collection Management*, *37*(2), 98–109. http://dx.doi.org/10.1080/01462679.2012.656554.

Spalding, H. H., & Wang, J. (2006). The challenges and opportunities of marketing academic libraries in the USA: experiences of US academic libraries with global application. *Library Management*, *27*(6/7), 494–504. http://dx.doi.org/10.1108/01435120610702477.

Staiger, J. (2012). How e-books are used. *Reference & User Services Quarterly*, *51*(4), 355–365.

Staley, D. F., & Malenfant, K. J. (2010). *Futures thinking for academic librarians: Higher education in 2025*. Retrieved from http://www.ala.org/acrl/sites/ala.org.acrl/files/content/issues/value/futures2025.pdf.

Steer, D., & McConnell, D. (2008). Evaluating higher order thinking skills in large general education geology courses for non-majors. *Abstracts with Programs – Geological Society of America*, *40*(6), 306.

Stevens, N. D. (2006). The fully electronic academic library. *College & Research Libraries*, *67*(1), 5–14.

Stewart, C. (2012). Preservation and access in an age of e-science and electronic records: sharing the problem and discovering common solutions. *Journal of Library Administration*, *52*(3/4), 265–278. http://dx.doi.org/10.1080/01930826.2012.684505.

Stielow, F. (2011). Accreditation, ROI, the online academic library. *Computers in Libraries*, *31*(9), 6–9.

Stillman, L., & Linger, H. (2009). Community Informatics and information systems: can they be better connected? *Information Society*, *25*(4), 255–264. http://dx.doi.org/10.1080/01972240903028706.

Strothmann, M., & Antell, K. (2010). The live-in librarian: Developing library outreach to university residence halls. *Reference & User Services Quarterly*, *50*(1), 48–58.

Stueart, R. D., & Moran, B. B. (2007). *Library and Information Center Management*. Westport, CT: Libraries Unlimited.

Su, S. S. (2006). Individual learning and organizational learning in academic libraries. In C. Khoo, D. Singh, & A. S. Chaudhry (Eds.), *Proceedings of the Asia-Pacific Conference on Library & Information Education & Practice 2006*. Singapore: School of Communication & Information, Nanyang Technological University.

Taber, A., & Conger, M. (2010). Relevance recognized: value-added cataloging for departmental and digital collections. *Cataloging & Classification Quarterly*, *48*(6/7), 585–601. http://dx.doi.org/10.1080/01639374.2010.496311.

Tan, S. C. M., & Higgins, S. E. (2002). *Library as a learning organization*. *Libri*. NTU (Nanyang Technological University), 169–182.

Tang, R. (2004). Evolution of the interdisciplinary characteristics of Information and Library Science. *Proceedings of the American Society for Information Science and Technology*, *41*(1), 54–63.

Taylor, N. (2008). Metaphors, discourse, and identity in adult literacy policy. *Literacy*, *42*(3), 131–136.

Tennant, R. (2001). XML: the digital library hammer. *Library Journal*, *126*(5), 30–32.

Tenopir, C. (2010). Measuring the value of the academic library: Return on Investment and other value measures. *Serials Librarian*, *58*(1–4), 39–48. http://dx.doi.org/10.1080/03615261003623005.

Tharani, K. (2012). Collections digitization framework: a service-oriented approach to digitization in academic libraries. *Partnership: The Canadian Journal of Library & Information Practice & Research*, 7(2), 1–13.

Thinking outside of the library box: the library communication manager. *Serials Librarian*, *53*(3), (2007), 17–39.

Thomas, T., Davis, T., & Kazlauskas, A. (2007). Embedding critical thinking in IS curricula. *Journal of Information Technology Education*, 6827–7346.

Tinto, V. (2006). Research and practice of student retention: what next? *Journal of College Student Retention*, *8*(1), 1–19.

Torabi, N. (2011). Academic libraries should consider a strategic approach to promotion and marketing of e-books. *Evidence Based Library & Information Practice*, *6*(4), 130–133.

Torff, B. (2003). Developmental changes in teachers' use of higher order thinking and content knowledge. *Journal of Educational Psychology*, *95*(3), 563–569. http://dx.doi.org/10.1037/0022-0663.95.3.563.

Trifonas, P. P. (2000). *Revolutionary pedagogies: Cultural politics education and discourse of theory*. Psychology Press.

Tyson, L. (2011). The future of the image in critical pedagogy. *Studies in Philosophy & Education*, *30*(1), 37–51.

Ubogu, J. O., & Okiy, R. B. (2011). Sources of funds in academic libraries in Delta State, Nigeria. *Library Philosophy and Practice*. Retrieved from http://unllib.unl.edu/LPP/uboku-okiy.htm.

Um, A. Y., & Feather, J. (2007). Education for information professionals in the UK. *The International Information & Library Review*, *39*(3), 260–268.

UNESCO. (2005). *Beacons of the information society: The Alexandria proclamation on information literacy and lifelong learning*. Retrieved from http://www.unesco.org/new/en/communication-and-information/access-to-knowledge/information-literacy/.

Updike, C. B., & Rosen, A. L. (2006). Integrating digital technology into teaching: the MDID. *Art Libraries Journal*, *31*(3), 32–36.

Varalakskhmi, R. S. R. (2009). Future of library and information centres in knowledge society. *DESIDOC Journal of Library & Information Technology*, *29*(2), 75–81.

Vasileiou, M., & Rowley, J. (2011). Marketing and promotion of e-books in academic libraries. *Journal of Documentation*, *67*(4), 624–643. http://dx.doi.org/10.1108/00220411111145025.

Vasileiou, M., Hartley, R., & Rowley, J. (2012). Choosing e-books: a perspective from academic libraries. *Online Information Review*, *36*(1), 21–39. http://dx.doi.org/10.1108/14684521211206944.

Vaughn, D., & Callicott, B. (2004). Broccoli librarianship and Google-bred patrons, or what's wrong with usability testing? *College & Undergraduate Libraries*, *10*(2), 1–18.

Virkus, S. (2003). Information literacy in Europe: a literature review. *Information research*, *8*(4), 4–8.

Vucovich, L. A., Gordon, V. S., Mitchell, N., & Ennis, L. A. (2013). Is the time and effort worth it? One library's evaluation of using social networking tools for outreach. *Medical Reference Services Quarterly*, *32*(1), 12–25. http://dx.doi.org/10.1080/02763869.2013.749107.

Walter, S. (2005). Moving beyond collections: academic library outreach to multicultural student centers. *Reference Services Review*, *33*(4), 438–458. http://dx.doi.org/10.1108/00907320510631562.

Watanabe, Y. (2007). How to promote e-resource services in academic libraries. *Journal of Information Processing & Management/Joho Kanri, 50*(6), 343–353.

Waterman, R. H., Jr. (1992). *Adhocracy: A form of organization that cuts across normal bureaucratic lines to capture opportunities, solve problems, and get results.* New York.

Weiner, J. (2011). Is there a difference between critical thinking and information literacy? A systematic review 2000–2009. *Journal of Information Literacy, 5*(2), 81–92.

Welch, J. M. (2005). The electronic welcome mat: the academic library Web site as a marketing and public relations tool. *Journal of Academic Librarianship, 31*(3), 225–228.

Whitmire, E. (1998). Development of critical thinking skills: an analysis of academic library experiences and other measures. *College and Research Libraries, 59*(3), 266–273.

Williams, H., & Peters, A. (2012). And that's how i connect to my library: how a 42-second promotional video helped to launch the UTSA libraries' new Summon mobile application. *Reference Librarian, 53*(3), 322–325. http://dx.doi.org/10.1080/02763877.2012.679845.

Williams, N., Bishop, A., Bruce, B., & Irish, S. (2012). Community Informatics for whom? *Journal of Education for Library & Information Science, 53*(3), 218–221.

Williams, R. (2003). *Higher order thinking skills: Challenging all students to achieve.* Thousand Oaks, CA, US: Corwin Press.

Wilson, T. (2010). Information sharing: an exploration of the literature and some propositions. *Information Research, 15*(4), 12.

Wittwer, R. (2001). Special libraries–how to survive in the twenty-first century. *The Electronic Library, 19*(4), 221–225.

Wolski, M. (2011). Building an institutional discovery layer for virtual research collections. *D-Lib Magazine, 17*(5/6), 1–9. http://dx.doi.org/10.1045/may2011-wolski.

Worthey, G. (2009). "Long live the corpse!" At-risk open-access humanities journals in LOCKSS. *Against The Grain, 21*(1), 22–26.

Wu, C. C., & Chiu, M. H. P. (2011). Development of information ethics in library and information science in Taiwan. *Journal of Library and Information Studies, 9*, 123–156.

Wu, M. M. (2011). Building a collaborative digital collection: a necessary evolution in libraries. *Law Library Journal, 103*(4), 527–551.

Xia, Z. (2009). Marketing library services through facebook groups. *Library Management, 30*(6), 469–478. http://dx.doi.org/10.1108/01435120910982159.

Ye, Y. (2009). New thoughts on library outreach to international students. *Reference Services Review, 37*(1), 7–9.

Yi-Chu, L., & Ming-Hsin, C. (2012). A study of college students' preference of servicescape in academic libraries. *Journal of Educational Media & Library Sciences, 49*(4), 630–636.

Ying, Chau, M. (2006). Connecting learning styles and multiple intelligences theories through learning strategies: an online tutorial for library instruction. *LIBRES: Library & Information Science Research Electronic Journal, 16*(1), 5.

Zachary, L. J. (2011). *Creating a mentoring culture: The organization's guide.* John Wiley & Sons.

Zambare, A., Casey, A., Fierst, J., Ginsburg, D., O'Dell, J., & Peters, T. (2009). Assuring access: one library's journey from print to electronic only subscriptions. *Serials Review, 35*(2), 70–74. http://dx.doi.org/10.1016/j.serrev.2009.03.002.

Ziaei, S., & Nooshinfard, F. (2012). Evaluation of central libraries' websites of universities in Iran from a marketing viewpoint. *Libri, 62*(3), 276–290.

Zimmerman, D., & Paschal, D. (2009). An exploratory usability evaluation of Colorado state university libraries' digital collections and the Western Waters digital library websites. *Journal of Academic Librarianship, 35*(3), 227–240.

Zohar, A., & Dori, Y. J. (2003). Higher order thinking skills and low-achieving students: are they mutually exclusive? *The Journal of the Learning Sciences, 12*(2), 145–181.

Zorich, D. M. (2007). Preservation and access for a digital future: the WebWise Conference on Stewardship in the digital age. *Curator, 50*(4), 455–460.

# INDEX

*'Note*: Page numbers followed by "f" indicate figures and "t" indicate tables.'

Printed in the United States
By Bookmasters